# TEACHING THINKING

## A Survey of Programmes in Education

# Teaching Thinking

A Survey of Programmes in Education

EDITED BY M.J. COLES
& W.D. ROBINSON

BRISTOL CLASSICAL PRESS

First published in 1989 by The Bristol Press,
an imprint of Bristol Classical Press

This second edition published in 1991 by
Bristol Classical Press
an imprint of
Gerald Duckworth & Co. Ltd.
The Old Piano Factory
48 Hoxton Square, London N1 6PB

A catalogue record for this book is available
from the British Library

ISBN 1-85399-277-1

Printed in Great Britain by
Billing and Sons Ltd., Worcester

# CONTENTS

# INTRODUCTION TO THE SECOND EDITION

The term 'cognitive science' was coined to refer to what members of a number of otherwise distinct disciplines – philosophers, psychologists, neurologists, students of artificial intelligence, as well as educationalists – were converging upon, namely, an interest in thinking. The American term 'critical thinking' is widely used to refer to a transformation of a great deal of this theoretical and descriptive work into a series of practical and normative programmes which aim to teach more effective thinking. The present volume represents a selection of those programmes represented in Britain.

It will be noticed that here there is no one agreed name for the ideal, though several suggestions are offered. We would like to make our own. Since the aim of these programmes is not simply to describe thinking but to prescribe norms of thinking, we suggest 'effective thinking' as a more positive term than 'critical thinking' and also less likely to be confused with the completely different 'critical theory'. Since the aim is also practical, perhaps 'teaching effective thinking' would best suit the ways of reaching the ideal.

There are two main emphases in this volume. The first is on practice. Two essays are an exception to this: the first chapter highlights some theoretical issues, and the essay by Greg Hunt casts serious doubts on the possibility of the whole enterprise, doubts which have to be faced if the movement these programmes represent is to have any plausibility. The second emphasis is on what is happening in Britain. Again there are some exceptions: the essay by Alec Fisher on critical thinking records how it arose in North America, where it has made its earliest and greatest advances, against which scene the position in Britain may be seen in more adequate perspective; the chapter by Michael Whalley describes how the 'Philosophy for Children' programme – used by a number of individual teachers in Britain – originated in the USA; and John Nisbet relates the movement in Britain to developments that have been taking place in other parts of Europe and the world.

Apart from those exceptions the objective of this volume is to bring a range of practical programmes, at present operating in

1

Britain, to the notice of educational practitioners, administrators and politicians, as well as teacher-educators, other academics and the public at large. It was not practicable to include those programmes which aim to teach effective thinking but have a base within discrete subjects, e.g. the many new science syllabuses.

Apart from the influence of the Thinking Skills Network, the programmes dealt with in this book operate in Britain largely in isolation from each other. Also, until recently they operated without public recognition. However, in late 1990, BBC2 screened 'The Transformers', a series of films on the art of inspired teaching, featuring the work of Lev Vygotsky, Reuven Feuerstein and Matthew Lipman. To date, ten thousand requests have been received for the supporting booklet. To our knowledge, over four hundred people wrote for information or materials concerning just one of the teaching programmes. They divide almost equally between, on one side, parents wanting for their children something they suspect schools are not regularly providing, and, on the other side, teachers who say this is what they have always wanted to provide but are prevented from doing so by pressures mostly generated for non-educational reasons. 'Transformers' clearly touched a nerve and revealed a need.

It is hoped that the surprising – and gratifying! – rapid sell-out of the first edition of this book indicates an increasing awareness of the need to develop more creative thinking and interest in the possibilities of achieving it. This second, updated, and enlarged edition is offered as a further contribution to the growing British literature on the subject.

In Chapter 1 we review some of the critical questions which have to be addressed by those considering the general field of teaching thinking. It will be noted that one of the characteristics, shared by discussion within the various programmes designed to teach more effective thinking, is the addressing of these same questions at various levels. It may be wondered whether there is a certain self-destructiveness about these considerations, if they give rise to the view that all theoretical questions must be settled and overall agreement reached before a programme or programmes are entertained by schools or educational authorities. In particular, the demand for positive, evaluative results before a programme is launched may prohibit the very evaluative study which could provide those results. Understandable and advisable as it may be not to commit resources to something untried, there exists, as we try to indicate, sufficient evidence of the positive effects of teaching thinking programmes to warrant more attention to them than is currently being given in the British educational and political establishment as a whole.

Programmes that are introduced, however, should have a sound theoretical base and be recognised as addressing *inter alia* the questions we have identified.

It was the editors' intention to include in the first edition of this book an overview of British education, identifying several general tendencies hospitable to a growing emphasis on the teaching of thinking. Sadly, this intention came to nothing, so leaving an unfortunate gap in our perspective. **John Nisbet** has written a new chapter for this second edition which not only fills this gap but also adds further dimensions. While noticing several issues which we also raise in Chapter 1, in Chapter 2 he places them in the wider contexts of a) a worldwide movement of research and application, b) general aspects of the British educational scene, and c) specific movements of both theory and practice throughout the European mainland. This last-named dimension will be of increasing importance after 1992.

It will be seen that Nisbet tends to favour infusion of teaching thinking across the curriculum, over against the special-subject approach. Although, as he maintains, it is questionable as to how far results of the special-subject approach will enable the skills of thinking to transfer to other subjects and into 'real life', we must also ask whether the infusion model gives sufficient identity to the teaching of thinking for it to resist dilution by the pressures of crowded syllabuses. Also, can education achieve balance without a deliberate timetable slot in which the synthesis of separate subjects is deliberately addressed? Special-subject *and* cross-curricular infusion in mutual support may well be the ideal aim.

In his book *Critical Thinking and Education* (Oxford 1981) – curiously more influential in Britain than in the Americas where its central theses have been widely criticised – John McPeck claimed that there are no general skills of thinking. Although strongly in favour of more attention to the deliberate teaching of effective thinking, he believed that the specificity of knowledge required that this be done within the context of the subject disciplines. Some may see **Greg Hunt**'s contribution to this book as an updating into the computer age of this serious objection to teaching thinking as presently conceived. Several issues, however, are in need of clarification. The thesis that there are no general inferential rules of thinking apart from logic leaves open the question of what exactly is being included and excluded from logic.

Many would claim that even if logic were to include only the rules of formal logic then this would be a necessary and powerful addition to the curriculum of, at the latest, the upper secondary school. A project which attempted to introduce just such an addition and which ran from 1975 to 1988 is described by **Humphrey Palmer**. He explains how The Cardiff Project was initiated and carried through, and why it failed to expand. In doing this he implicitly offers advice about the practical difficulties of setting a curriculum innovation in motion, and notes the problems of maintaining momentum in the present educational climate.

The Cardiff Project attempted to introduce sixth-formers to traditional and symbolic logic. Others would wish to address the general rules of thinking which may not be strictly inferential at all but without which thinking is ineffective: such rules as learning to formulate fecund questions, trying to see at least two sides to any question, and the 'social' rules of careful, empathetic listening and respect for other people's opinions. Others again might wish to explore those wider understandings of 'logic' which Hunt says are not yet in an advanced state of development. Both these aspects are the subject of Informal Logic, identified in other parts of this book. Perhaps a more general worry will be raised by Hunt's paper: Is there a sufficiently strong analogy between human thinking and artificial thinking to justify the argument that since computer simulations of human thinking cannot do x, y, z, therefore humans cannot (ought not to) do x, y, z?

In any case, it could be that the whole argument has been falsely formulated by those who see it as a competition between the teaching of factual knowledge and the teaching of skills. (A similar, simplistic polarisation now threatens to bedevil the subject of teacher training.) Alternatively, it might be seen as an appeal for a better balance between the teaching of subject-specific knowledge and the teaching of those intellectual skills which are found to be enhanced by metacognitive activity, some of which may turn out to be more general than is suggested by the traditional subject-discipline demarcations. Hunt's views come as a timely warning against too facile a view of this balance.

In Chapter 5 on Critical Thinking, **Alec Fisher** mentions the multiplicity of texts available, and states that 'nearly all of these are North American so far', modestly omitting reference to his own major contribution, *The Logic of Real Arguments* (Cambridge University Press 1988). He sketches some of the historical background of the emergence of this movement, pointing to three examples which differ widely in their approach. It is not insignificant that all of them emphasise the desirability of fostering rational and independent thinking, and that the context is the perceived slump in thinking skills, identified as a major political and educational danger some decades ago in the USA where democracy – at least in theory – prizes those skills.

The subject which has traditionally been the locus of self- conscious thinking about effective thinking is philosophy. Although this has for some time been present informally in many British schools – particularly in the non-state sector – there has been a widespread reluctance to recognise its appropriateness at sub-degree levels. The recent advent of philosophy as a formal qualification at A-level – offered by both the Associated Examining Board and the Joint Matriculation Board (who now also offer an A/S-level) – coheres with the view of those who repudiate this reluctance. Among those knowledgeable in this particular field, **Dermot O'Keeffe** is highly respected both as a member of the AEB Philosophy Group and as a sixth form teacher of distinction. His essay presents details of the syllabuses available as well as discussing theoretical and practical problems of the actual teaching involved. It is interesting to note that philosophy at this level is slowly winning recognition among professional philosophers, even gaining an honourable mention in the University Grants Commission's recent review of the subject!

'Philosophy A-level', says O'Keeffe, 'is baptism by total immersion', and there are those who will wonder about the dangers of drowning would-be converts! Do the syllabuses do much to advance the cause of the teaching of effective thinking as an entitlement of *all* students at that level, let alone at earlier levels? The weight of textual and historical material, and the course format's similarity to many undergraduate programmes, might suggest that this is yet more content-bound learning, translatable into exercises in critical and creative thinking by only a very small elite. On the other hand, it was essential that the A-level should be seen to have the rigour necessary to satisfy higher educational entrance requirements. Now that it has received widespread university recognition, modifications are possible, to give greater space to the skills of thinking over against textual knowledge, as the syllabuses come up for review, but these will have to face the vexed problems of appraisal which O'Keeffe notes.

Professor Matthew Lipman's 'Philosophy for Children' is a programme based on the conviction that thinking philosophically is the right of, and within the capability of, every schoolchild. In Document B2 1394/87, the European Parliament recommended it to the European Commission as a programme which 'gives concrete expression to and clearly reflects the recommendations and guidelines set out in the Community's own documents dealing with education'. It is now recognised as an educational tool of enormous potential in many countries of the world. Yet **Michael Whalley** explains that it will disappoint anyone who hopes for an educational tool for moulding children into some adult conception of what 'good thinkers' should be. This is because it has an uncompromising insistence that children have a right to develop their own philosophical thinking. In discussing the key aim, Dr Whalley raises questions about the nature of teaching, and the nature of children as learners, which have to be addressed by any programme that attempts to teach effective thinking – questions which the Philosophy for Children programme tries to answer via its distinctive methodology. The Philosophy for Children programme was developed in the USA, and there are practical problems attached to the attempt to use the programme in Great Britain. The novels which act as a stimulus for discussion have a strong American flavour and many here feel the need to adapt them to British culture, but the depth and richness of its many dimensions can easily be lost in this kind of translation. More importantly, the distinctive methodology is a crucial element in the programme, since one of its key aims is the development of a 'community of enquiry' through classroom dialogue. Orchestrating a truly philosophical discussion is a difficult art to master, and mechanisms for the training of teachers and parents are only now being set up in this country, largely in response to interest in 'The Transformers'.

A point of interest to many in **Keith Jackson**'s essay will be that it is an approach partly rooted in industry. There are those who fear the business orientation that is being forced on the educational system by present political and economic pressures, seeing the profit-motive as inimical to sound scholarship. Signs exist, however, of an awakening in industry to the necessity of developing our people's highest potential intelligence if we are to succeed in *any* sphere, not least the economic. Already, projects to enhance employee performance are bearing an interesting likeness to some of the 'teaching thinking' programmes; perhaps not surprisingly, as investigation into their respective roots reveals earlier cross-fertilisation.

Jackson's insistence that the problems and solution-methods are already with us may be seen as a further example of the suggestion that the creation of self-consciousness concerning the process of effective thinking is a first essential step towards the enhancement of that process. Some may see his recommendation 'to ask the pupils what we should think about when we want to get results' as a reference to the most crucial – and perhaps the most pedagogically difficult – point at issue. Other essays in this book might well be seen as addressing the questions of exactly how and when that question can be successfully raised. That it should be raised, however, and that raising it and getting pupils to answer it puts them into a position of greater control over, and enhancement of, their own intellectual abilities – this appears to be central to the whole enterprise.

A pioneer in this field – though somewhat apart from the North American tradition – is Israeli psychologist Reuven Feuerstein, whose programme 'Instrumental Enrichment' (IE) is discussed in the chapter by **Bob Burden** and **Anton Florek**. Feuerstein, like Lipman, emphasises the quality of the teacher's role in facilitating students' own learning how to learn. The complementary emphasis, however, that no one at any age is beyond the possibilities of improving their intelligence, should come as welcome news as well as a challenge to teachers and parents. The quality of our own thinking about thinking is just as important as – indeed, is inextricably involved in – our teaching children how to think, and stands alongside the need for appropriate teaching materials. Feuerstein's term for the adult's role is 'mediation'. However, in these days when students from a very early age have access to processes and vast stores of information beyond the limits of their teachers, mediation should not be understood to mean simply 'filtration'; Burden and Florek's 'dynamic filter' captures this point. They therefore join other writers in urging adequate personal resourcing of teachers in this field.

Instumental Enrichment has been influential in Britain, largely through spin-off from its trial by five educational authorities in the early eighties. Two of those authorities (Oxfordshire and Somerset) perceived the need to draw on the theory and practice of Feuerstein and others for a whole range of pupils, and to do so through indigenous programmes.

A particular point of interest in **John Hanson**'s account of the Oxfordshire Skills Programme is the contention that psychometric evaluation may not be as relevant in this field as 'anecdotal' reporting. Teacher evaluation in particular may be peculiarly appropriate here. It is noteworthy that one of the most widely recognised effects of introducing programmes such as Feuerstein's, and those based in part on Feuerstein, has been the effect on the teacher's self-image and self-understanding of her role. This does not preclude a formalisation of such evaluations, and several attempts are in hand in that direction. However, the point emphasises the importance of the teacher modelling in her own thinking and relationships whatever it is that she is trying to nourish in her pupils. One should not be surprised if an early and reliable indication of the effectiveness or otherwise of a programme is the effect it has on the teacher.

John Hanson also makes explicit the political context briefly mentioned above. The British context is that of a parliamentary democracy which – in ideal at least – works through citizens being able to exercise rational judgement. There are many worries today that rational argument is being replaced by the packaging and marketing of opinions. Behind all the programmes presented in this book lies belief in the value of maximising the judicious and rational thinking of our people. Politicians of the right may see effective thinking in terms of performative efficiency, especially in an increasingly competitive world. Those of the left may see these programmes as a 'democratisation' of educational opportunities. But all believers in parliamentary democracy may recognise the moral and political dangers of neglecting those abilities which this volume considers.

The Somerset Thinking Skills Course incorporates a wide range of theoretical backgrounds, of modes of presentation, and of skills, dispositions and attitudes. There is also careful attention given to transfer from real life *into* the lessons as well as transfer and generalisation *out* of them. The course is published by Basil Blackwell. It is to be hoped that, in spite of publication, schools and teachers who contemplate using it will not lose sight of the emphasis laid by **Nigel Blagg** and **Marj Ballinger** on the need for in-service induction and refreshing. It is also to be hoped that the material will not be ossified by print but open to emendation through experience of its use. It is already expected that the methodology will be further applied to lower and higher educational phases, in particular in connection with the National Curriculum and the parallel concerns within business and industry.

In spite of the work of the Thinking Skills Network, the programmes described have remained isolated both from each other and from the mainstream of educational life in this country. Yet, in Professor Nisbet's view, 'by the beginning of the twenty-first century, no curriculum will be regarded as acceptable unless it can be shown to make a contribution to the teaching of thinking'. In commending these programmes and their respective methodologies to more serious consideration in Britain, we can only point to the many other countries that are currently seeking to maximise their people's greatest resource – their *potential* intelligence – and urge attention to John Hanson's final question: 'Why haven't we a national programme?'

# 1: TEACHING THINKING: WHAT IS IT? IS IT POSSIBLE?

## M.J. Coles and W.D. Robinson

No one doubts, theoretically, the importance of fostering in school good habits of thinking. But apart from the fact that the acknowledgement is not so great in practice as in theory, there is not adequate theoretical recognition that all which the school can or need do for pupils, so far as their minds are concerned...is to develop their ability to think.

John Dewey

In recent years there has been increasing attention given to the idea that schools should be less concerned with imparting information and more concerned with encouraging the kind of teaching which pays attention to the way children learn. There has, too, been an increasing realisation that children's thinking abilities are underestimated. Margaret Donaldson's critique and reinterpretation of Piagetian theory (Donaldson 1978) is just one example of work which suggests that previous assumptions about children's limited capacity for reasoning and abstract thought are inaccurate (e.g. Brown and Desforges 1979, Modgil and Modgil 1982).

These ideas have allowed a great explosion in the number of attempts at teaching thinking directly. The essays in this book describe such attempts. They are clearly evidence of a significant intellectual movement, one in which a great deal of thought and energy is being expended.[1] But the range of programmes described is also evidence of an ever-increasing number of strategies and definitions. Different conceptions of what one is trying to achieve in teaching thinking have led to clusters of different approaches to the task. A number of questions apply to all these approaches.

There is the question of what teaching thinking means. This is not merely a matter of definition, but a question which requires consideration of a number of substantive issues. Does teaching thinking mean imparting skills? What are these 'thinking skills'? Can teaching thinking concentrate on skills alone or must attention be given to the disposition to use such skills? How can a teaching thinking curriculum do this? Crucially, do thinking abilities require knowledge of specific disciplines and so are in some sense domain-specific, or can thinking abilities and dispositions transfer across domains? Can the ability to think well be taught via a context-free curriculum?

Answers to these questions will be part of the answer to the question 'Is it possible to teach thinking?' It might be thought that the range of programmes described in this book and the evidence offered by the writers suggest a positive answer is obvious. However, to ask whether thinking can be taught at all is not the same as to ask whether it can best be taught using this or that methodology, and the answers to these questions can raise further queries which must in turn be met.

There is also the question of how teaching thinking is justified. Why should teaching thinking programmes be introduced into schools? While it may seem obvious to many that teaching thinking is an important educational desideratum, it is still the case that teaching thinking programmes need to offer reasons why they should be considered for inclusion in the school curriculum. On the face of it this presents a problem, since the variety of teaching thinking programmes might be criticised as a confusion of educational aims and curriculum agendas.

Certainly the different methodologies are the outcome of a variety of justifications, educational, political and philosophical.[2] This does not mean, however, that they are necessarily opposed. A number of approaches have overlapping justifications, and common elements. It is not the purpose of this chapter to provide a summary of the reasons given for teaching thinking, but it is important to understand that the several perspectives in recent developments in teaching thinking are, in part, the result of differing justifications.

The essays in this volume are evidence that there is no single approach to teaching thinking. But if there is no consensus about what exactly teaching thinking should be, there are certainly clear candidates for elements to be included in any teaching thinking curriculum, and if the idea of teaching thinking is to carry any weight in educational thinking and practice, then it is important that we define some parameters, so that we know what we are talking about when we talk of the desirability of teaching thinking. Quite clearly there is little point in setting out to teach thinking unless one has a reasonably clear conception of one's objectives. So what are these parameters?

## What is 'teaching thinking'?

Let us admit immediately that it is difficult not to become confused with regard to the diversity of behaviours that are classifiable as thinking. The thinking process is a vast and intricate family of activities: there is thinking as one speaks, as one writes, as one plays, as one dances etc. Unfortunately when thinking is defined in this way, so as to apply to all distinctively human behaviour, it becomes useless as a word to utilise for the purpose of making distinctions within such behaviour. We could help ourselves, perhaps, by asking what kind of thinking is of particular relevance to education and to the programmes which purport to teach it. Even so, the inventories of types of thinking which would then be produced may still cause us to think we are dealing with something unmanageable.

However, it is possible to offer some categorisation that begins to make sense of this variety. First, there is the classic distinction between making, saying and doing. One way to start categorising the types of thinking which the programmes attempt to teach might be to ask whether or not the programmes depend on literacy. Not all thought is dependent on language, as Gilbert Ryle's examples of thinking which requires experience and practice but not language show: 'The architect might try to think out his design for the war memorial by arranging and re-arranging toy bricks on the carpet; the sculptor might plan a statue in marble by modelling and remodelling a piece of plasticene.' So some teaching thinking programmes ask participants to use imagination and play with ideas in drawing in order to gain a feel for the way in which a projected hypothetical idea works. After all, the inability to describe a plan in words does not necessarily mean that no plan has been developed.

Nevertheless, though thinking is not all done with language, that is usually how it is usually conveyed, recorded and taught. Since linguistic communication is the primary vehicle of education, most teaching thinking programmes centre their attention on language.

So what other categorisations are there that may help analyse the types of thinking to which teaching thinking programmes pay attention? A useful one has been devised by Robert Sternberg (1987). He divides thinking skills into three kinds:

1. Executive processes which are used to plan, monitor and evaluate one's own thinking.

2. Performance processes which are used actually to carry out that thinking.

3. Learning processes which are used to learn how to think in the first place.

Examples of executive processes would be identifying and form-ulating a question, keeping the situation in mind and organising thoughts. Performance processes are such things as seeing similarities and differences, deducing, and making value judgements. Asking and answering questions of clarification such as 'What do you mean by that?', and listening carefully to other people's ideas, are examples of learning processes. One could ask then if, and how, the different programmes attempt to teach these different kinds of thinking as a way of discovering what type of thinking they value.

If we did this we would certainly identify within the range of programmes what might be called the 'pure skills' conception of teaching thinking. According to this view teaching thinking is a matter of teaching a list of skills. Such skills might include the ability to ask relevant questions, being able to see connections between different strands of thought, the ability to distinguish relevant from irrelevant considerations, skill in evaluating conflicting courses of action, the ability to think analogically, skill in detecting fallacies in reasoning, being able to give reasons for beliefs held and decisions made, the ability to generalise from particular instances, drawing out the con-sequences of what is said and done (inferring), and so on.

Such a pure skills conception of teaching thinking does not solve the problem that the list of thinking skills is potentially very long indeed. Lipman (1983) has pointed out that 'thinking skills' is a catch-all phrase:

> It ranges from very specific to very general abilities, from pro-ficiency in logical reasoning to the witty perception of remote resemblances, from the capacity to decompose a whole into parts to the capacity to assemble random words or things so as to make them well-fitting parts of a whole, from the ability to explain how a situation may have come about to the ability to foretell how a process will likely eventuate, from a proficiency in discerning uniformities and similarities to a proficiency in noting dis- simi-larities and uniquenesses, from a facility in justifying beliefs through persuasive reasons to a facility in generating ideas and developing concepts, from the capacity to solve problems to the capacity to circumvent them or forestall their emergence, from the ability to evaluate to the ability to reenact – the list is endless because it consists in nothing less than an inventory of the intellectual powers of mankind.

This is, it must be admitted, a huge obstacle to teaching thinking despite the potential for categorisation discussed above. But if one is convinced that a concentration on teaching thinking holds out the promise of dramatically improving education then it is an obstacle which must be overcome. Perhaps this is best done by admitting the impossibility of teaching all thinking skills, and then by identifying and utilising those approaches to teaching thinking which involve children in an educational process; a process in which not a comprehensive range, but a wide spectrum of thinking skills are sharpened in an educationally significant fashion.

There may of course be an explanation for the inconclusiveness of categorisation. Sternberg gives a clue to one possible explanation when he draws our attention to the varying levels of conscious attention. Perhaps taxonomies of thinking skills are as difficult as Lipman suggests because there is about them a kind of recursiveness, so that at whatever level one looks at a particular thinking skill there is a more primitive level at which all the thinking skills may be seen in that one. For example, if one were to list x, y, z as the skills of problem solving, it might be possible to analyse x again in terms of x, y, and z, and so on. It becomes a matter of which level one chooses to analyse the processes.

But teaching thinking cannot mean only imparting particular skills, for that would sanction our regarding people as skilled thinkers even though they may never, or only rarely, use the skills. Most programmes, realising this, admit that a set of tendencies is required. Proficiency is not enough: there must also be a tendency to exercise that proficiency. Most programmes work on the basis that one must not only teach skills but one must also encourage the disposition to use them. Richard Paul, an advocate of the critical thinking movement, is a leading exponent of this view, a view he explains in the following passage, more fully quoted by Alec Fisher in his contribution to this volume:

> ...we become rational...to the extent that our beliefs and actions are grounded in good reasons and evidence...to the extent that we have cultivated a passion for clarity, accuracy and fairmindedness. These global skills, passions, dispositions, integrated with a way of acting and thinking, are what characterise the rational, the educated and, in my sense, the critical person. (p. 6)

So teaching thinking must take dispositions into account. These dispositions are not themselves skills, but they do represent a readiness to use them. Examples of such dispositions, which are both cognitive and affective in nature, would be respect for persons, readiness to consider alternative explanations, care for the procedures of inquiry; readiness to listen to others, a habit of judicious suspension of assent and a habit of self-appraisal. Lipman (1983) sums up lists like these of habitual dispositions with the term 'commitment to inquiry'; McPeck (1981) calls this tendency to behave in a particular way on particular occasions 'reflective scepticism'.

Maybe, then, we ought not to be talking about skills at all, but about capacities. Smith (1987) puts the point this way:

> Regarding capacities as skills may be a way of insisting on their separateness from personality: the 'real me' is not put at risk by rebuff or failure if it is only my skills that are found wanting...My skills do not testify to the kind of person I fundamentally am ...Our skills do not say much about who we are because they make no reference to our dispositions, our wantings and valuings, and it is by virtue of these that we are persons of one sort or another. (p. 5)

Certainly we ought to take care when talking of thinking skills that we do not suggest that skills can somehow be appended or tacked on to people, nor suggest that such skills are in a sense entities themselves, almost as if they could exist in their own right independent of persons. But talk of 'capacities' to add to the other terminology – 'dispositions', 'habits', 'tendencies' etc. – perhaps confuses rather than makes clear what we wish to refer to. Our preference is for the following definitions:

Skills – the particular abilities.

Dispositions – tendencies to use those skills in appropriate situations.

Attitudes – a certain delight in using the skills.

Using these definitions one can see that Richard Paul seems to be referring to both dispositions and attitudes in the above quotation.

Whatever terms we use, what are the factors which determine whether appropriate thinking is demonstrated generally? What factors do teaching thinking programmes have to take into account to ensure that dispositions and attitudes are acquired? Well, one of the most important must be self-concept or self-image. There is now a general consensus that the way pupils feel is related to the manner in which they perform in the classroom, and there are numerous findings which suggest that high self-esteem is a necessary pre-condition for achievement (e.g. Purkey 1970; Lawrence 1973; Huntingdon and Ross 1981; Gammage 1982; Lane and Lane 1986). We are unlikely to behave in particular ways, to acquire particular dispositions and attitudes, if we do not see ourselves as the kind of person who behaves in these ways. Similarly, children are unlikely to test and demonstrate their ability to think in particular ways and in particular circumstances if they do not believe that such thinking is either possible or permissible for them. Frank Smith (1984) has described this factor as the feeling of being a member of the club:

Experienced members of the club demonstrate all the club activities to new members...there are no prerequisites for membership...just mutual unqualified acceptance. The child and the more experienced club members see each other as the same kind of people. It is taken for granted on both sides that the child will learn, but also that not everyone will be as experienced and practised as everyone else. (p. 6)

The social context in which teaching thinking takes place is then of major importance. Lipman (1983) explains the crucial relevance of the social context for the teaching of thinking thus:

Inquiry is, to a considerable extent, predicated upon the operation of a self-correcting community. One learns to think objectively by recognising the viewpoints, perspectives and reasoning of others, and by proceeding to entertain the attitude of the entire community towards the projects in which all participants are involved. It is only when the classroom is conducted by recognised search procedures and by open exploration of the issues that cognitive skills are employed in ways which develop inquiry dispositions among participants while furthering the inquiry itself. (p. 8)

Here, then, are other defining questions one might ask about teaching thinking programmes. How far do the programmes take into account that the teacher may act as a thinking and social model? What account do they take of the social situation in which learning takes place? What if, as Vygotsky has suggested, children are capable of functioning intellectually at a higher level when in collaborative or co-operative situations than when they are required to work individually? It does seem that if teaching thinking is to be successful it must realise that thinking capacities are grounded in both cognitive and affective aspects of people. And if teaching thinking is regarded as an educational ideal which must take into account character traits, dispositions and habits of mind as well as particular skills, it should not then become undervalued as just another skill area. Rather, a skills, dispositions and attitudes conception of teaching thinking construes it as a fundamental ideal, and a movement for educational reform, which should inform the entire range of educational activities and affairs.

*What is the best approach?*
The notion that teaching thinking should be a fundamental educational ideal gives rise to two further basic questions. The first has both theoretical and pedagogical import and is quite crucial for the programmes described: Are the skills, dispositions and attitudes so far

identified general characteristics or are they necessarily subject-specific? Secondly, if they are general, are they best taught via discrete programmes or should they be infused into subject areas? These two questions are obviously related, since the second only arises if the characteristics are general, but they should not be confused because it is conceivable that, even though general thinking skills exist, they are best taught through the diffusion rather than the discrete model.

The theoretical objection to general thinking skills was put by McPeck in his influential book *Critical Thinking and Education* (1981), and is clearly the question which underlies Greg Hunt's article in this volume. McPeck argues that all thinking is evaluated by the standards of some specific subject. He maintains that the only way to teach thinking is through a given field, learning the subject matter and methods of that field. He argues thus because he holds that thinking cannot be regarded properly as a generalised skill since there is not any one skill that can be applied generally across subject area domains.

At the pedagogic level many teachers would confirm McPeck's view by suggesting that they are teaching thinking by the very act of teaching their subject. They would agree that it is not enough simply to learn the contents of a discipline; that pupils must learn to think in that discipline, to think historically, mathematically or scientifically; but the route to this goal, according to this view, lies in identifying the reasoning and inquiry skills appropriate to the practice of individual subjects and then teaching such skills.

Now it cannot be denied that most disciplines make a wide range of cognitive demands upon those who study them. A list of typical classroom questions provides evidence of the variety of patterns of thinking to which pupils are required to respond: 'What does the word "approximate" mean?', 'In what ways do mammals and reptiles differ?', 'Why are days longer in the summer?', 'How would you prove that these triangles are equal?', 'Why did Guy Fawkes plan to blow up the Houses of Parliament?' However, though it is reasonable to argue that good teachers in all subjects encourage their pupils to think, this is not the same as teaching them how to think – for instance, by explicitly drawing their attention to the kind of thinking they are engaged in. Teaching thinking means providing not just encouragement and opportunity, but a knowledge of principles and techniques and regular guided practice in applying those principles and techniques.

Further, although it is often the case that specialist knowledge is needed to determine the correctness of a point of view, or the accuracy of an analysis, or the feasibility of a plan, it is also the case that there are common extra-disciplinary standards of good thinking. There are errors common to many fields, and thinking in a given domain is not immune to criticism from outside that domain. Siegel (1988) has noted the weakness in McPeck's thesis. He points out that McPeck fails to take seriously obvious examples of general, i.e. not subject-specific, skills and abilities, and confuses specific acts of thinking with thinking conceived as a general capacity which includes specific acts or episodes as instances. Govier (1988) provides the kind of examples that Siegel has in mind, and reinforces his point: 'A question-begging argument is as wrong in history as it is in physics and for the same reasons...the idea that clarity, inference, presentation, even overall cogency are completely relative to and internal to the various disciplines is descriptively implausible and normatively inadequate.' (p. 32)

There are still more rejoinders to the McPeck point of view. As is regularly pointed out by commentators on this topic, thinking *in* a subject is not the same as thinking *about* a subject. The discipline-specific approach does not enable children to forge links between different areas of knowledge, thus offering the opportunity to make sense of the disparate school curriculum; nor does it offer children the chance to examine the nature of their own thinking, as some teaching thinking programmes are designed to do.

Suppose it were agreed that general skills of thinking exist, there remains the second practical problem of how they are best to be taught. Different chapters in this volume represent different views on this question. There are difficulties with each approach. If we concede that we ought to leave the responsibility for teaching thinking solely in the hands of teachers of the traditional disciplines, granting that they will attempt, for instance, to emphasis the nature and importance of considering one's own thinking, then we come up against difficult pedagogic problems. The goal of having teachers focus attention on their pupils' thinking while at the same time instructing in their disciplines would inevitably lead to a tension between teaching thinking and dealing with the direct topic, whatever it might be. Robin Barrow (1981) offers one example of this problem:

> There is a distinction between stating clearly 'what I mean by democracy is one man one vote' in order to advance a discussion in a history lesson about whether Periclean Athens was or was not democratic, and attempting to analyse the concept of democracy which would involve one in a more painstaking task which would have nothing specifically to do with Athens. (p. 135)

Perhaps this tension would be no bad thing, for it would lead us to question the emphasis of our educational efforts. If the primary aim of education is conceived to be the promotion of children's thinking, then knowledge acquisition has to assume a subsidiary status and thinking must not be taught only as a subcomponent of other activities. Thoughtful pupils will, more often than not, be able to inquire after and locate the knowledge they require, while the converse may not be the case.

On the other hand, in the present British educational climate, finding resources of time, teacher expertise and funding for discrete courses of teaching thinking has its own obvious problems.

One might ask, though, whether there really is any need in practice to choose between two approaches which may not be incompatible with each other. Perhaps the model of contest is unnecessary and schools do not need to choose between discrete teaching thinking programmes or infusion into the current cur- riculum. Sternberg (1987) has realised that it is possible to argue for a mixed model in which thinking skills are taught in separate courses as well as being infused into the entire curriculum. This model would meet objections from both sides of the debate. A mixed model would not simply assume that context-free approaches could teach thinking in isolation, thinking which might then be plugged into particular disciplines if and when required; nor would it rely on those disciplines independently to come up with curricula or pedagogies which put the ideals of teaching thinking into practice. Rather, it would imply a cross-fertilisation between discrete programmes and the traditional disciplines so that teaching thinking programmes would act as a catalyst to influence the pedagogy and curriculum of the whole school, and that curriculum would in turn provide subject matter for the discrete programmes. In this respect we might think of teaching thinking as analogous to teaching writing. All pupils need specific specialist teaching in learning how to write for a variety of audiences and a variety of purposes, but at the same time facility in writing cannot be developed and maintained unless it has continued attention in all curriculum areas.

### Does 'teaching thinking' work?

Proposing such a model for teaching thinking does not affect the fact that there is, in the educational community, a good deal of scepticism about the notion that you can teach thinking at all. Such scepticism proceeds in part from a misconception about what is meant by teaching thinking, but also from the false assumption that if teaching thinking is not being taught and has not been taught, then it cannot be taught. It is the fallacy of reasoning from 'didn't' to 'couldn't'.

The scepticism is not entirely invalid, though, for a major concern in any discussion of teaching thinking programmes must be the question of evidence and validation. If it is stated, for instance, that children who have been taught to be systematically inquisitive and reflective, in a special programme designed to do just that, tend to import such behaviour into their other learning activities, then the inevitable response is that whether such a statement is correct or not needs to be judged in the light of suitable educational experiment and measurement. The blunt statement 'It is possible to teach thinking' is an empirical one and so ought to be backed by empirical evidence.[3]

There are some who consider that the seeking of such evidence may lead us in the wrong direction. They hold the view that teaching thinking ought not to be justified only in terms of the success of the enterprise, by reference, for example, to its instrumental function in relation to improving performance in the disciplines. Teaching thinking, they say, is a humanistic endeavor which represents an enrichment of the individual that needs no other justification.

Nevertheless, and recognising this point of view, it is still the case that if teaching thinking is to be a goal of education and therefore to call for changes in current practice, then most people – politicians, administrators, parents – would want to see some evidence that such changes will be effective. There is little point in setting out to teach thinking, these people might say, unless one has some effective way of judging whether or not one has been successful and whether one's approach does lead to an obvious improvement in pupils' thinking.

Now it may be the case that if research carried out in schools into the effectiveness of teaching thinking programmes does not provide evidence for the improvement of thinking capabilities, this may be because teachers presently have no more expertise in this area than pupils, or because a particular programme is not well designed, or simply because the research is inadequate. For example, should attempts be made to measure thinking capabilities solely through individual tasks, if we know that enlisting children's social impulses results in improved cognitive performance? The complex nature of the capacity that teaching thinking attempts to develop is such that it is easy to appreciate the difficulties of creating a way to measure progress towards this development. So lack of evidence could not be taken as a watertight case against the possibility of teaching thinking in schools.

As it happens we do have evidence, partly gained from evaluations of the programmes documented in this book, that it is possible, in schools, to improve the abilities and attitudes associated with thinking. There is evidence to show that teaching thinking programmes will, in some measure, increase such things as pupils' powers of judgement, reasoning, memory, attention and motivation.

The most comprehensive evaluations have been of Feuerstein's Instrumental Enrichment Programme and the Lipman Philosophy for Children material. Both these programmes have been extensively tested, revised and evaluated, and have been shown to work in a number of different settings. The results of extensive evaluations of the programme devised by the Institute for the Advancement of Philosophy for Children (Lipman and Shipman 1979) is summarised by Lane and Lane (1986) thus:

> The results indicated a significant improvement in formal reasoning and in creative reasoning (the capacity to generate new ideas, to discover feasible alternatives, and to provide reasons). The overall impact of the programme in improving reading and mathematics was also found to be significant. The teacher's appraisal was that children were markedly more curious, better oriented towards their work, more considerate of one another, better able to reason, and that their communication skills increased. (p. 265)

Lane and Lane also note other evidence that the programme can lead to improvements in formal and informal logic, critical thinking, fluency and flexibility of thought, reading, interpersonal relationships and social skills (Burnes 1981, Curtis 1980, Haas 1976, Higa 1980, Karras 1980, Shipman 1982, Yeazell 1981). They point out that the most positive result seems to have been in terms of children's view of themselves as thinkers who ought to be taken seriously by adults as well as other children (Curtis 1980).

Clearly we ought not to underestimate the cognitive abilities of even very young children, especially considering the enormous feats of learning achieved before they even start formal education. But as is clear from the results of evaluations such as those above, quantitative criteria which relate to cognitive skill improvement as measured by tests are not the only relevant ones. Qualitative criteria which relate to the educational significance of the approach used – how it helps to achieve the aims of teaching thinking – must be taken into account. And the interdependence of these two types of judgement must be recognised because what the evaluator chooses to measure can be as significant as the result of any particular evaluation. As the earlier discussion pointed out, teaching thinking means taking account of the fact that good thinkers display particular dispositions and attitudes as well as a wide range of cognitive skills and strategies evidenced in contexts as diverse as philosophical inquiry and practical problem solving.

There is, too, evidence from experiments in psychology which have no direct connection with teaching thinking programmes, and which explore the possibility of teaching thinking outside the school context. Here, although there are still a large number of open questions, there is also a large amount of evidence which can help us to evaluate teaching thinking programmes, for certain lines of inquiry offer the suggestion that certain approaches to teaching thinking are likely to be more successful than others.[4] In particular this research has led to an improved understanding of the importance of meta-cognition. The importance of addressing one's own thinking has long been recognised. Alfred Binet, the developer of intelligence testing, believed self-criticism to be a central factor in intelligence, a factor that is not inborn but must be nurtured. Gradually this understanding has been confirmed and reinforced. It is now realised that good thinkers have acquired a recognition of the need for self-knowledge and self-control of learning and problem-solving strategies. But this is not a matter of innate cognitive abilities; rather it is a matter of being given the opportunity to acquire particular capabilities. Perceived differences in the intellectual functioning of different individuals may well be the result of the different opportunities those individuals have had to develop capabilities in the organisation and management of their own learning.

Teaching thinking can help such development by enhancing the tactical repertoire that pupils can draw on in their thinking and by offering the opportunity to look explicitly at that repertoire. Super-ordinate, or what were earlier called executive strategies, pay for themselves, as Perkins (1987) has pointed out, 'not so much during the week or month in which they are acquired as during the years that follow. Like compound interest, they increase the learner's intellectual capital. The tactic "try to make up a tactic and use it" is a simple example.'

Belmont, Butterfield and Ferranti (1982) have reviewed seven studies which provide evidence that important transfer of thinking skills can be achieved if general tactics, or executive skills, such as goal-setting, planning and self-monitoring are 'trained' as well as more specific cognitive skills:

> These facts suggest that the deliberate training of superordinate processes will result in important gains in the ability...to think productively and to solve novel problems. To the extent that productive thinking and novel problem-solving signify intelligence, we may be confident that intelligence can be modified by

attending to children's superordinate self-management skills. It is unknown how much improvement can be expected, but we suppose that cognitive researchers have barely scratched the surface. (p. 153)

When Edward Glaser published his famous work *Experiment in the Development of Critical Thinking* in 1941 he listed over 340 scholarly books and articles, all of them either documenting that thinking can be taught or explaining how and why to teach it. The studies quoted in this chapter are part of a huge corpus of work that has grown in the five decades since Glaser's book and extended our knowledge of the possibilities of teaching thinking.[5]

The problem now is not whether we can teach thinking. The evidence suggests we can. The problem continues to be whether we are willing to make the pedagogical changes necessary to do so, and if we are, which changes might be the most effective.

*Notes*

1. Other evidence for this fact came at a conference organised by the OECD Centre for Educational Research and Innovation (CERI) in July 1979, the purpose of which was to discuss and advance the state of our knowledge about how young people think and reason, reported in McLure, S. and Davies, P. (1991), *Learning to Think: Thinking to Learn*, Pergamon Press.

2. For a categorisation of the various justifications offered for teaching thinking see Anthony Blair's 'Recent Developments in Critical Thinking in Anglophone North America', *Thinking*, Vol. 7, No. 2, 1987, pp. 2-6.

3. The problems of obtaining such evidence via tests are discussed by T.N. Tomko and R.H. Ennis in Blair, J.A. and Johnson, R. (eds) (1980), *Informal Logic: The First International Symposium*, California, Edgepress.

4. An excellent summary of research in psychology which has implications for teaching thinking is contained in Perkins, D.W., 'Thinking Frames: An Integrative Perspective on Teaching Cognitive Skills', in Baron, J. and Sternberg, R. (eds) (1987), *Teaching Thinking Skills*, New York, W.H. Freeman.

5. For a comprehensive collection of recent work in this field see Chipman, S.F., Segal, J.W. and Glaser, R. (1985), *Thinking and Learning Skills*, New Jersey, Lawrence Erlbaum.

*Bibliography*

Baron, J. and Sternberg, R. (eds) (1987), *Teaching Thinking Skills*, New York, W.H. Freeman.

Barrow, R. (1981), *The Philosophy of Schooling*, Brighton, Wheatsheaf Press.

Belmont, J., Butterfield, E. and Ferretti, R., 'To Secure Transfer of Training Instruct Self-Management Skills', in Detterman, D. and Sternberg, R. (1982), *How And How Much Can Intelligence Be Increased*, USA, Ablex.

Brown, D. and Desforges, C. (1979), *Piaget's Theory: a Psychological Critique*, London, Routledge.

Burnes, B. (1981), 'Harry Stottlemeier's Discovery – The Minnesota Experience', *Thinking*, Vol. 3, No. 1, pp. 68-70.

Curtis, B. (1980), 'Philosophy for Children in Hawaii', *Thinking*, Vol. 1, pp. 52-6.

Dewey, J. (1916), *Democracy and Education*, New York, Macmillan, p. 179.

Donaldson, M. (1978), *Children's Minds*, London, Fontana.

Gammage, P. (1982), *Children and Schooling: Issues in Childhood Socialisation*, Allen and Unwin.

Glaser, E. (1941), *Experiment in The Development of Critical Thinking*, New York, Columbia University Press.

Govier, T., 'Ways To Teach Reasoning Directly', in Fisher, A. (ed.) (1988), *Proceedings of the First British Conference on Informal Logic and Critical Thinking*, University of East Anglia.

Haas, H.J. (1976), 'Results of the 1975 Experimental Research in Philosophy for Children at Newark, Rutgers University, Institute of Cognitive Studies', *Institute for the Advancement of Philosophy for Children Report*.

Higa, W.R. (1980), 'Philosophy for Children in Hawaii', *Thinking*, Vol. 2, pp. 21-31.

Huntingdon, P. and Ross, E. (1981), 'Self-Concept in the Classroom', *European Journal of Social Psychology*, Vol. 10, No. 2, pp. 70-82.

Karras, R.W. (1980), 'Final Evaluation of the Pilot Programme in Philosophical Reasoning in Lexington Elementary Schools', *Thinking*, Vol. 1, pp. 26-32.

Lane, N.R. and Lane, S.A. (1986), 'Rationality, Self-Esteem and Autonomy through Collaborative Enquiry', *Oxford Review of Education*, Vol. 12, No. 3, pp. 263-75.

Lawrence, D. (1973), *Improved Reading Through Counselling*, Ward Lock.

Lipman, M. and Shipman, V.C. (1979), 'Summary of Results of 1976-78 Experimental Research in Philosophy for Children: Newark and Pompton Lakes', *Institute for the Advancement of Philosophy for Children Report.*

Lipman, M. (1983), *Thinking Skills Fostered by Philosophy for Children*, Institute for the Advancement of Philosophy for Children.

McPeck, J. (1981), *Critical Thinking and Education*, Oxford, Martin Robertson.

Modgil, S. and Modgil, C. (1982), *Jean Piaget: Consensus and Controversy*, Eastbourne, Holt, Rinehart and Winston.

Paul, R., 'Critical Thinking and the Critical Person', quoted in Fisher, A. (ed.) (1988), *Proceedings of the First British Conference on Informal Logic and Critical Thinking*, University of East Anglia, p. 6.

Perkins, D.N., 'Thinking Frames: An Integrative Perspective on Teaching Cognitive Skills', in Baron, J.B. and Sternberg, R.J. (eds) (1987), op. cit.

Ryle, G. (1955), 'Thinking and Language', *Aristotelian Society Supplementary Volume XXV,* p. 69.

Shipman, V.C. (1982), 'Evaluation of the Philosophy for Children Programme in Bethlehem, Pennsylvania', *Thinking*, Vol. 4, pp. 37-40.

Siegel, H. (1988), *Educating Reason*, London, Routledge.

Smith, F. (1984), *Learning to be a Critical Thinker*, Canada, Abel Press.

Smith, R., quoted in Holt, M. (1987), *Thinking Skills in the Curriculum*, paper presented to the inaugural meeting of the Thinking Skills Network, Chester, 25.4.1987.

Vygotsky, L. (1978), *Mind in Society*, Cambridge M.A., Harvard University Press.

Yeasell, M.I. (1981), 'A Report on the First Year of the Upsbur County, West Virginia, Philosophy for Children Project', *Thinking*, Vol. 3, pp. 12-14.

# 2: PROJECTS, THEORIES AND METHODS: THE INTERNATIONAL SCENE

## John Nisbet

Though the focus of this book is on developments in Britain, it is important to place them in an international context. The explosion of interest in the idea of teaching thinking is world-wide. In countries throughout the developed world, the curriculum in schools is being modified to develop skills of problem solving, critical reasoning and creative thinking: not just memorising factual knowledge but learning how to use that knowledge to deal with problems, adapting to new situations, learning to plan ahead and work on your own or co-operatively in small groups.

The greatest volume of publications on this theme has come from the USA and Canada. In the USA currently, there are over one hundred programmes on the market which claim to teach thinking; almost all colleges and universities offer courses on thinking skills; there are computer programs and games, and a flood of books, videos and tapes, in-service courses and conferences on this topic. There are several comprehensive reviews of American work readily available, with critical discussion of the issues involved (for example, Baron and Sternberg 1987; Nickerson 1988; and the April 1988 issue of the American journal, *Educational Leadership*).

In Western Europe, there is research in Belgium, Finland, France, Germany, Greece, Italy, Portugal, Spain, Sweden and Britain. Much of this work is essentially psychological, but examples of educational programmes will be described later in this chapter. There are no comprehensive reviews of the European work comparable with the American reviews mentioned above. A journal article by McGuinness and Nisbet (1991) concentrates mainly on the underlying psychological frameworks adopted in various European approaches. An earlier review of Dutch and German research (Beukhof and Simons 1986) is now rather out of date; and the conference proceedings of EARLI (the European Association for Research on Learning and Instruction) (Mandl *et al.* 1989), though a rich source of ideas, tend to be too specialised to be helpful for teachers.

There are parallel developments in the countries of Eastern Europe and the USSR, which are attracting growing interest. In Australia too, there are centres of research and development in this field in Adelaide, Brisbane, Melbourne and Sydney.

In addition, there is a world-wide 'Philosophy for Children' movement, which aims to translate the procedures and concepts of logic and ethics into practical issues which can be worked through in discussion with children. Examples from Britain are described in Chapter 7; other examples are mentioned later.

The growing use of computers in schools, for problem-solving, simulations, information processing and retrieval, has added further interest in the possibility of teaching thinking. In many countries, professional training courses in management, business studies, medicine and law are increasingly concerned with problem-solving and decision-making processes and critical thinking, using case studies, simulations and a problem-orientated approach.

### The problem-solving approach

The most significant evidence of change, however, is probably not to be found in these specially designed programmes or courses on thinking, nor in developing information technology. It is to be seen in the adoption of a problem-solving approach within the traditional subjects of the curriculum, both in primary and secondary education. This too is a world-wide trend, particularly in science and mathematics, and it is the approach which tends to be favoured in Britain.

The idea is not new in primary education: the 'progressive education' movement emphasised the need for children to be active participants in their own learning, and the 'project method' is widely used in primary schools to involve pupils in thinking things out for themselves. In secondary education, revised syllabuses for the GCSE in England and SCE in Scotland include projects or 'investigations' which aim to develop enquiry and problem-solving skills, not only in science and mathematics but also in other subjects such as history and geography. This change is not without controversy; some of those who support the idea see it primarily as the way towards better understanding of the subject, while others aim at developing transferable skills. Official policy is still sceptical of teaching general thinking skills. [The National Curriculum Council set up a Task Group to consider learning and thinking skills as a cross-curricular theme, but nothing has been officially heard of their deliberations at the time of writing. – eds] The Scottish report on mathematics (SED 1990), for example, approves the problem-solving approach but emphasises that 'It is not a question of spending time on this rather than on other components of the curriculum; these skills can be developed while concepts, facts and techniques...are being acquired and consolidated'. Perhaps the trend is more evident in the rhetoric than in the reality; for the pressures of overcrowded syllabuses and the demands of examinations compel many teachers to concentrate on teaching the knowledge content of their subjects, and students resort to memorising factual information. There is no time for thinking – sometimes not even for understanding!

*The constructivist view of learning*

We can hardly accept this as a satisfactory state of affairs. The demand for a 'Thinking Curriculum' arises partly because of rapid changes in modern society. It is also the result of recent developments in cognitive psychology: the constructivist theory of learning argues that learners create their own frameworks of interpretation in a search for meaning and understanding. Learning is not just a product of teaching: it requires an active effort of understanding and compre- hension by the learner. Knowledge without understanding is limited: it is too easily forgotten, it cannot be readily retrieved when needed, it becomes quickly out of date in a period of rapid change, and it can be applied only in the context in which it was learned, so that it is ineffective in novel situations. If learning is to be retained and to be readily available for use, learners must make their own construction of knowledge – make it their own – and must learn to take responsibility for the management and control of their own learning.

The ability to monitor our thinking, and consciously to apply strategies to manage and control it, is the key to teaching thinking. The idea of teaching thinking is not new. From Plato down the centuries, improving the intellect has been a prime educational aim. In the nineteenth century, the study of Latin and mathematics was seen as a 'mental discipline' to strengthen the 'faculty' of reason. This 'faculty' theory was discredited early in the twentieth century, and it was replaced by a theory of inborn intelligence, which determined whether we could think and how well. But the constructivist approach, which sees learners as active creators of their own knowledge and their own frameworks of interpretation, casts doubt on the belief that inborn intelligence is the sole determinant of individual differences. The recent growth of information technology – information processing and retrieval, artifical intelligence and the use of computers – has supported this development by giving us a vocabulary of concepts such as 'executive and non-executive processes' (explained in Chapter 1): executive processes manage the mental operations of the non-executive knowledge content in thinking. This has opened up the possibility of teaching these executive processes.

Thinking is a process which we have to learn. We build up our own personal frameworks of interpretation and understanding, and techniques of problem solving, through experience. A rich culture like ours offers many of these frameworks ready-made, in language, mathematics and science, for example; but each of us has to make these frameworks our own. There are skills and strategies in thinking which we build from experience: the mastery of these skills need not be left to chance – they are too important for that. Some people are quicker than others at acquiring these skills; but appropriate teaching can help all of us to improve our competence.

## Programmes versus infusion

When it comes to methods of achieving these aims, the main division is between those who aim to teach thinking skills through separate courses, specially designed, and those who favour the infusion of thinking throughout the established subjects of the traditional curriculum.

Those who adopt a 'skills' approach identify component skills in thinking and practise these skills through exercises which are usually 'content-free', or not closely linked with any one subject discipline. There are many of these programmes available: in the USA, they often have dramatic names – Talents Unlimited, HOTS (Higher Order Thinking Skills), Project Impact. De Bono's CoRT and Feuerstein's Instrumental Enrichment are among the best known – and they are being tried in many countries, including China. The main criticisms of this approach (though this does not apply to all of them) are that it treats thinking as an 'add-on' element, that the skills approach is 'reductionist' or fragmentary, and that transfer of these skills to new contexts is limited. Teachers are often sceptical of whether the skills taught in these programmes transfer to other domains of thinking. They do contain good advice: stop and think, define the problem, break it into stages and tackle them one at a time, look for possible analogies, consider contrary evidence as well as the evidence that supports your assumptions, and so on. But knowing the rules does not guarantee that you will apply them or know which to select or how to combine them into effective strategies.

The infusion approach means embedding the teaching of thinking within the established curriculum. Thinking is not an 'add-on' but an integral element in the teaching and learning of all subjects. Learning is not just acquiring masses of information; but it isn't just doing 'problems' or 'investigations' or 'projects' either. Infusion involves teaching the process of thinking together with the content of knowledge. The balance of opinion seems to favour this approach, reflected in the slogan, 'The Thinking Curriculum'.

*Methods*
Within this latter approach, it is possible to list a range of methods which have been extensively tried and tested. These include modelling, questioning, discussion and co-operative learning.

In modelling, the teacher talks aloud while working through a problem or composing a letter or report. She makes her strategies explicit in discussing how she tackles the task, as a model for the pupils – and also to show that experienced thinkers often come to dead ends but are able to recognise and deal with dead ends when they do come to them. For example, this can be used in drafting written text, or in revising a draft to edit it. The teacher's commentary must consist of much more than simple procedural instructions: she must be aware of her own thinking processes, so that the children can see how she responds emotionally and intellectually to the task, how she sets about establishing a suitable working procedure, how she marshalls information and searches her memory for relevant points, how she copes with distractions, the stress of time limits, and so on. Obviously, it is not sufficient to do this only once and expect the children to master what is involved. It must become a regular part of the teacher's repertoire.

Questioning is another technique which is familiar to all teachers. The skill is in knowing what questions to ask – or rather, what *kind* of questions to ask. Richard Paul, an American authority on critical thinking (whose work is explained in Chapter 5), recommends a form of Socratic questioning: Why do you say that? Can you explain? Are there arguments against? Questions like these are designed to make children think, and to make their thinking explicit.

Discussion is another well-established method. In teaching thinking, discussion involves the analysis of argument and the reasons underlying conclusions and assertions. Discussion of this kind requires a climate of openness in the classroom, the teacher's role being to bring ideas into the open, not to instruct authoritatively on what is right or wrong.

Co-operative learning is a fashionable phrase for children working together in pairs or in small groups. There are many ways in which it can be applied in teaching thinking: for example, one child explains to another how to tackle a problem, and in talking his thoughts aloud he makes his thinking clear (to himself, if not to the other child!) and focuses attention on the process of thinking. Co-operative learning allows strategies to be shared and discussed, so that students learn from each other's errors, and from their own.

These are not new methods: teachers will recognise them as familiar techniques for involving pupils in their own learning. But here they are used in a special way, and for a special purpose; and teachers need practice and training in using them in this way. The common element which runs through all these methods when they are used for teaching thinking, is metacognition – developing awareness and control of your own thinking processes. The American psychologist, Glaser, describes it as 'internalising self-regulating strategies': learners must 'take over' from their teachers the control and management of their thinking processes.

### The teacher's role

Teachers have always set problems for children as part of their lessons; but often they omit to teach the children how to go about solving the problems. Perhaps, therefore, the first task is to train (or persuade) the teachers.

The role of the teacher in the process may best be described as that of 'mediator' (to use a term introduced by Feuerstein). The teacher mediates children's development by providing tasks appropriate to their stage of development and helping them to become aware of the strategies and procedures involved in tackling these tasks. The Russian psychologist, Vygotsky, suggested the concept of 'the zone of proximal development': this refers to a situation where a child cannot yet do something unaided, but can do it with help from a teacher (or from another more capable child). With the help of 'scaffolding', they can learn to do the task independently, and thus their progress through the stages of intellectual development can be accelerated.

### Examples from Europe

These ideas are being taken up in various projects throughout Europe. The approach to critical thinking through the teaching of philosophy, associated with Lipman and Paul (see Chapters 5 and 7), has attracted interest in several countries. In Spain, the Institut per l'Ensenyament de la Filosofia in Barcelona is translating some of Lipman's curriculum materials into Spanish; training courses for teachers and experimental work in primary schools are under way. Books on related topics (e.g. Nisbet and Shucksmith 1986) have been translated into Spanish. In Sweden also, the National Board of Education is funding a programme to use translations of Lipman's stories.

In Portugal, Project Dianoia (Learning to Think) at the University of Lisbon aims to promote thinking skills in school tasks such as text comprehension, written composition and science problem-solving; classroom lessons on training metacognitive awareness in these tasks have been successfully introduced.

In Finland, a programme on The Formal Aims of Cognitive Education (FACE) aims to help teachers to adapt their teaching, to encourage students in the analysis of thinking, the formation of concepts, deductions and inference. (These are the 'formal' aims of instruction, as distinct from the content aims or subject matter.) The formal aims are brought to students' attention by questioning techniques which they put to the teacher, to each other and to themselves.

At Gothenburg University in Sweden, Marton and his colleagues have shown how students' perceptions of the learning process influence the actual learning strategies which they deploy. Marton's 'deep' and 'surface' levels of processing provide a structure for analysis which has been widely adopted – for example, by Entwistle in Britain, and Biggs and Ramsden in Australia.

In France, the traditional curriculum with its emphasis on language and (in senior classes) philosophy and logic is seen by many as the most effective route to teaching thinking. But other approaches are also being tried: for example, Caillot's work on problem solving in science and computer programs for teaching thinking; Barth's methods to strengthen concept formation; and Debray's description of the use of Feuerstein's Instrumental Enrichment with disadvantaged adolescents in Paris.

In England, the project Cognitive Acceleration through Science Education (CASE), is an example of teaching thinking processes through the established curriculum. Though a science-based programme, it aims to develop general thinking skills as well as scientific reasoning. Initiated in 1984, it is now at the stage of yielding encouraging evaluation results which show that many pupils after two or three years in the programme perform significantly better not only in science but also in mathematics and English.

These are only a few of the projects and publications in European countries. There is a strong network of researchers in the Netherlands, an active centre of research in Leuven, Belgium, and extensive research and development in Germany and other countries. (References for the examples quoted are given in McGuinness and Nisbet 1991, and Nisbet and Davies 1990.)

Nor is this work confined to Europe and North America. In Australia, for example, Philosophy for Children is promoted through a centre at the Australian Council for Educational Research and fourteen regional groups; Flinders, Melbourne and Monash Universities all have active researchers in this field; and State Departments of Education in New South Wales, Queensland and South Australia have teams developing materials and in-service courses.

*Key issues*

In the concluding section of this chapter, four themes are identified as key issues for research and development: transfer, attitudes, evaluation and assessment.

Whatever method is adopted, the crucial test of the effectiveness of the method is transfer – whether competence acquired in one context can be applied in a different context. Too often it is assumed that if you teach children to solve mathematical problems, they will be better able to solve real-life problems. But real-life problems are 'fuzzy': it is often harder to identify what the problem is than to find a solution. Thus, teaching pupils to solve equations or puzzles, or to identify a logical fallacy, is merely teaching tricks, unless the strategies learned are more widely applied – for then it becomes teaching thinking. The general rule is to 'teach for transfer', demonstrating wider application and giving practice in related but different applications. Baron and Sternberg (1987) list six ways of maximising transfer, the first of which is to teach 'executive skills' – that is, metacognitive monitoring.

Attitudes and motivation play an important part in thinking, for thinking requires effort (cf. Coles and Robinson's 'dispositions' and 'attitudes' in Chapter 1). Knowing about effective thinking is not enough: we also have to want to use that knowledge and to develop the habit of thinking. Writing from the Netherlands, Boekharts (1988) distinguishes 'awareness' and 'willingness', using the example of a student who is aware of the strategy to use (for instance, double-checking a calculation or reading over a script) but in a balance of judgement is unwilling to make the effort required. Self-image influences the response to difficulty: if we see failure as due to lack of effort, we try harder; if we see it as due to our lack of ability, we give up; if we have been trained in metacognitive monitoring, we try a different strategy. Thus students' perceptions are all-important: their perceptions of the task, of the process, and of their own competence.

How are such attitudes acquired? Probably they are 'caught, not taught'; they develop from relationships and the examples of models whom we respect and admire. The social context of learning is therefore important, and the role of the teacher (or the parent) is to build these relationships, to set good models, and to establish an appropriate climate of learning. Positive attitudes to thinking are encouraged in a climate of learning which is tolerant of questioning and exploration, and are discouraged by an emphasis on memorising and an authoritative regime. So it is not just a matter of teaching skills and strategies, but rather one of creating 'powerful learning environments' (De Corte 1990) and 'communities of inquiry' (Lipman, see Chapter 7).

If people are to be persuaded to take teaching thinking seriously, there must be hard evidence that it can be done, that it achieves what it claims, that children and adults think more effectively as a result of instruction. Inevitably, this is difficult to prove. It is difficult to decide what should be taken as firm evidence of success: improved performance on IQ tests (or in exercises similar to those included in the programme of instruction) is not enough, since this may merely reflect a coaching effect. Nor can we readily distinguish between the merits of a programme and the methods used in applying it, or take account of the quality of teaching. Evaluation studies are inevitably short-term and cannot assess long-term effects. However, there has been fairly extensive evaluation of some of the specific programmes which claim to improve thinking (see Nisbet and Davies 1990). Not all these evaluations are sound: Nickerson (1988), in his review of the field, warns of 'unsubstantiated claims...one-sided assessments...excessive promotionalism'. Without more extensive long-term evaluation, there is a danger that band-wagon enthusiasm will end in a back lash reaction against the whole idea.

No proposal about curriculum or method can afford to ignore examinations. In secondary education, examinations have a strong influence on what is taught, how it is taught and how students set about their learning. Changing the examination system can be an effective means of influencing the curriculum; but if examinations emphasise the reproduction of factual information, they inhibit any approach based on problem solving and critical reasoning. The new examinations in Britain include provision for new forms of assessment which require the application of knowledge in tackling problems; but they do not indicate how pupils are to learn the necessary skills or how teachers should teach them. In the USA, the Educational Testing Service and other agencies are exploring modes of assessment which measure (and thus encourage) critical thinking. [See also proposals for a Higher Studies Test by the University of Cambridge Local Examinations Syndicate; Alec Fisher, University of East Anglia. – eds]

*Conclusions*

These and other issues are the subject of research and controversy among those working in countries across the world. One belief which they have in common is that the teaching of thinking is an important aim for education. Teaching thinking should not be seen as a new 'subject' battling for a place in an already overcrowded curriculum. The 'infusion' approach is a distinctive pedagogic strategy which affects all areas of the curriculum, implying a radical change of attitude to education, knowledge, teaching and learning. The need for this change is widely accepted: what it involves and how it can best be done, are still open to question. My own belief is that, by the beginning of the twenty-first century, no curriculum will be regarded as acceptable unless it can be shown to make a contribution to the teaching of thinking.

*Bibliography*

Baron, J.B. and Sternberg, R.J. (eds) (1987), *Teaching Thinking Skills: Theory and Practice*, New York, W.H. Freeman.

Beukhof, G. and Simons, P.R.J. (eds) (1986), *German and Dutch Research on Learning and Instruction*, Den Haag, SVO – Selecta Reeks.

Boekharts, M. (1988), 'Emotion, motivation and learning', *International Journal of Educational Research*, Vol. 12, pp. 229-34.

De Corte, E. (1990), 'Towards powerful learning environments for the acquisition of problem solving skills', *European Journal of Psychology of Education*, Vol. 5, pp. 5-19.

McGuinness, C. and Nisbet, J. (1991), 'Teaching thinking in Europe', *British Journal of Educational Psychology*, Vol. 61, No. 1.

Mandl, H., De Corte, E. Bennett, S.N. and Friedrich, H.F. (eds) (1989), *Learning and Instruction*, Oxford, Pergamon Press.

Nickerson, R.S. (1988), 'On improving thinking through instruction', *Review of Research in Education*, Vol. 15, pp. 3-57.

Nisbet, J. and Davies, P. (1990), 'The curriculum redefined: Learning to think – thinking to learn', *Research Papers in Education*, Vol. 5, pp. 49-72.

Nisbet, J. and Shucksmith, J. (1986), *Learning Strategies*, London, Routledge.

Scottish Education Department (1990), *Mathematics 5-14*, Curriculum and Assessment: A policy for the '90s (Working Paper No. 3), Edinburgh, HMSO.

# 3: SKILLS, FACTS AND ARTIFICIAL INTELLIGENCE

## G.M.K. Hunt

The teaching of logic and other inferential systems has a long history, and their systematic introduction into schools is to be applauded. But such an innovation should not be conflated with the change to 'skills based' syllabuses in, for example, History or Geography. This latter change presumes that there are general and pervasive inferential techniques which transcend subject boundaries and are a substitute for extensive familiarity with a particular subject.

In this paper I will draw on the experiences of research workers in Artificial Intelligence who have found from bitter experience that there are no domain-independent inferential rules which could be used to construct a general intelligence. This should not be interpreted as a narrow technical failure, but as an important general truth about the nature of human thought and the disciplines to which it is applied.

In a number of school subjects, particularly English, History and Geography, many syllabuses have been explicitly designed to foster the development of intellectual and practical skills. The aim here has been to develop in the student a battery of mental habits which will serve the pupil well, not only across the three subjects mentioned but in other subjects and in the wider world.

As pressures on timetable grow, the limited time available has forced a reduction in the factual content of these courses. Indeed, much factual learning has been derided as 'old fashioned' and its absorption educationally unnecessary, or at least of considerably less value than the skills of inference and judgement.

Much of this view, that there is a workable distinction between rules and facts, has been explicit during the last twenty years in Artificial Intelligence research. Part of the goal of this research has been to develop general purpose inferential techniques. These, it had been thought, could be applied to any selected body of factual knowledge to produce an artificial intelligence. As a result of much painstaking work, to be detailed below, it has become obvious that, apart from logic, there are no domain-independent inferential or judgemental rules. A considerable body of information about the topic must be supplied, in one way or another, and most of the inferences and judgements made draw in complex ways on this background information. To substantiate this point I will discuss three major subfields in Artificial Intelligence research, that is Expert Systems, Learning, and Dialogue Understanding.

*Expert systems*

Expert Systems are one of the few success stories of Artificial Intelligence research. Their development dates back to the 'General Problem Solver' of Simon and Newall of the late 1960s. Some have had remarkable success in narrow, well-understood domains; for example, 'Mycin' in medical diagnosis and 'Prospector' in geological exploration. It is not my purpose to belittle their success or to minimise the usefulness of them and their successors now coming onto the market. It is rather to draw attention to the nature of their weaknesses which differentiates them markedly, for many tasks, from human experts.

They consist, conceptually, of two parts: a data base of facts and relations; and an 'inference engine' which is applied to the knowledge base to derive further general, and particular, results.

The inference engine consists of the basic deductive rules of logic (often a more tractable, abbreviated form is used) augmented, usually, by a probabilistic or quasi-probabilistic inference system. Experience has shown that to achieve results capable of comparison with a human expert the inferences required need to go well beyond those of which Expert Systems are capable. We appear to need to be able to reject inferences made earlier – a requirement which is incompatible with deductive logic. Such so-called non-monotonic logics are not well understood and scarcely developed. In developing these logics, account has to be taken of the complexity of judgements made against a large and diffuse background of knowledge typically available to a human expert. As we shall see in discussing the knowledge base, it is difficult to represent this knowledge in a way that reflects its structure and makes it available in a form suitable for the inference engine.

In making inferences the system has not only to ensure correctness, but relevance. If this is not done systems soon bog down in a mire of unproductive activity. Some rules of guidance can be built into the system by appealing to 'Relevance Logics'. Such logics characterise the relations between propositions in terms of the interdependence of the truth between propositions. But there is a great doubt and dispute among developers of these as to which logic is best and for which purposes. More importantly, as research into scientific method has illustrated, what has appeared irrelevant to scientific investigation in one decade has become crucial in the next. To appraise a Relevance Logic one needs to understand the role and nature of judgements of relevance in the history of scientific expertise. We are far from having such an understanding.

From the point of view of the expert system, the knowledge base should consist of a set of propositions, many of relational form, which cogently comprehend the human expert's experience. Each proposition should have attached indication of the circumstances or limitations of its applicability and a measure of its reliability or relative certainty. To achieve this the expert is interrogated by a 'knowledge engineer' who attempts to propositionalise the expert's experience in a form suitable for use in the system. Success in this difficult task is variable; well-ordered narrow domains of knowledge are easier; large rambling domains are impossibly difficult.

To some extent the lack of structure and precision in the knowledge domain can be accommodated by representing the knowledge using so-called 'fuzzy logic', and building this capability into the inference engine as well. But again, not only is there much dispute over the various sorts of fuzzy logics, but even greater difficulty in knowing how to handle fuzzinesses which have quite different origins and causes in the expert's knowledge gathering process. For example, fuzziness which arises because of vagueness in some of the concepts in the field will have to be handled differently from fuzziness which arises from poor or missing experimental data.

Consider an example of the difficulties involved in replicating a simple mathematical deduction; that from $2 + 2 = 4$ to $2 + 3 = 5$. This deduction is only valid if one uses further information about the structure of the number system: that three is the successor of two and that five is the successor of four, as well as general rules about the behaviour of '$+$' and '$=$'. This involves an understanding of the general properties of the number sequence. There are many ways of representing the required information about numbers but none of them are simple, and turning this elementary inference into a valid logical deduction requires considerable background knowledge. Russell and Whitehead took almost one hundred pages to get this far in their logical analysis of mathematics. Yet it is difficult to see what a 'general rule' could be in this example if it wasn't the rule(s) of logic.

Less formal subjects such as History face much greater problems. Characterising beliefs is even less tractable. The inference from 'X thinks $2 + 2 = 4$' to 'X thinks $2 + 3 = 5$' requires a vast amount of background about X and the circumstances before it can be reduced to the simpler problem of the previous paragraph. Most rules of procedure in knowledge domains require an enormous background of knowledge and judgement specific to that domain before they become acceptable.

## Learning

What of learning? Can pupils be taught, or otherwise learn, general skills which enable them to learn in new knowledge domains? The difficulties faced by Artificial Intelligence research workers in the field of machine learning are instructive here.

Most current expert systems are static systems. They may infer new items of information, but they do not learn by interaction with their environment. A well-known Artificial Intelligence learning programme, the 'Arch Learning Programme' (Winston 1977), does learn in a small domain of children's blocks, with substantial help from the teacher.

The basic learning rule in the programme is reinforcement: consolidate success, try again after failure. The teacher presents examples both of arches and non-arches, built from children's blocks, and informs the machine whether its identifications are correct or not. Most of the detail is not important here but two matters stand out. The first is that, under favourable circumstances, the machine may learn the concept of an arch. But the associations between the geometric sub-concepts that are reinforced or destroyed by the examples presented, are supplied by the programme. It is only when these are appropriately relevant to the problem that learning takes place at all.

Equally important, the example of non-arches presented by the teacher must be 'near misses' or the machine simply goes off on a wild goose chase and learns nothing. Examples of 'not-the-concept' are essential to this sort of learning process. Before such a simple learning rule as is used in this programme has any chance of success, its application must be defined in terms of domain-specific sub-concepts to the appropriate field of knowledge. The rule, taken in isolation from domain-specific features, leads nowhere.

So the point is made again that there really is no general learning rule. What appeared to be a very general rule only has application and is given content by information about the domain of knowledge. This recurs again and again in Artificial Intelligence experiments. Without much domain-specific information, either built into the programme or supplied as a knowledge base, general learning machines thresh about and learn nothing. This is because the number of possibilities to be investigated multiply faster than the learning process prunes them away – a general fact known for many years.

It has been claimed (Dreyfus 1979, Gauld and Shotter 1977) that although some learning takes place in these toy worlds, real concepts are not just assembled from examples, but are open-ended in a way that makes it impossible to specify general rules for their manipulation in cognition. This claim has been strongly disputed, but if true would reinforce the claim of this chapter.

Let me now briefly discuss learning by discovery by considering Lenat's 'A.M.' programme (Lenat 1982) which was given the basic rules of arithmetic and, by heuristic means, was able to derive not just further mathematical truths but new and fruitful mathematical concepts. The invention (or discovery) of new concepts must be taken as a necessary component of any serious learning. The innovation in Lenat's programme came from the use of heuristic rules in an original way. Heuristic rules are essentially extra-logical rules of thumb which do not always work, but usually do in an appropriate context. They seem endemic in human thought.

Lenat built into his programme some basic heuristic rules, appropriate for the general subject matter, but allowed these rules to generate other heuristic rules, which generate further rules etc. The important feature which concerns us is the manner in which this is done.

Lenat provides the programme with some basic mathematical concepts and some basic heuristics. He arranged that concepts in the programme be held by filling slots in a general framework, one sub-frame for each concept. The slots contain information about the nature of the concept (e.g. the object has three sides) and its relation to other concepts (e.g. it is a sort of polygon). What is most important is that some of the slots are filled with heuristics which are applicable to that concept. That is, associated with each concept is a set of rules for manipulating that concept. It is these specific rules that give Lenat's programme much of its power.

The A.M. programme is considerably more economic and elegant than previous mathematical provers. It also generates many mathematical concepts which have proved so fruitful for human mathematicians. In doing so it provides further striking evidence for the thesis that productive inferential rules are closely related to the subject matter on which they operate, and that general rules are, in contrast, weak things which by themselves hardly contribute to understanding.

*Dialogue understanding*
Finally, a part of Artificial Intelligence which has generated much interest and support is Dialogue Understanding. This attempts to

produce a programme which comprehends prose to the degree necessary to produce a prose reply. Early attempts analysed the grammar of the sentence, no mean task in itself, then attempted to match the elements with a knowledge base. The performance reached by such machines was superficially impressive (Weizenbaum 1976) but quite inadequate for serious purposes. An interesting difficulty stood in the way of further progress. This was the need to involve the knowledge base in the grammatical analysis. Many ambiguities were thrown up by the grammatical analysis which could only be resolved by knowledge of the speaker's situation and the object(s) of reference. For example, the remark 'That's not what I ordered' can only be understood in a restaurant with the 'that' as referring to the contents of a plate rather than, say, the colour of the waiter's shirt.[1] This difficulty also forces each sentence to be analysed in the context of the preceding sentences. But context here means an appreciation of the flow of the discourse, which is not possible without knowing (or having an informed guess about) the purpose of the speakers, and this requires a knowledge beyond even the 'what and where' of information about restaurants and typical restaurant behaviour. Of course, in humans such knowledge is tacit, but the nature of Artificial Intelligence has forced it to be made explicit and in doing so shows that the deep grammar of discourse is interlinked with its content.

If the necessarily brief outlines of the evidence I have produced do convince, then it shows that the separation of general rules and skills from the content to which they are applied is very seldom successfully achievable, and only then in trivial contexts. The necessary background knowledge must often be absent in a syllabus which is short on content.

The experience of Artificial Intelligence research is important because to make a machine work at all, an instruction must be provided at each step. This provides a real test of the separability of skills from facts which is often missing in informal discussions of the issue. I am not arguing here that skills can never be taught, or that Artificial Intelligence has failed; rather that discoveries have been made which are important for a proper discussion of the teaching of skills in an academic context.

But teaching time is short and syllabuses are long. Not all the content of all courses can be taught in depth. The traditional solution is to teach a few courses in the requisite detail and hope that the experience of seeing the interlinking of skills and content will be transferred to the other subjects. Metaphors work this way; perhaps humans can manage the transfer on the grander scale, between subjects. But if they do, then it is by some process apparently different from the rules often invoked in a discussion of skills-based learning.

In a more positive note, although wholly compatible with the thesis argued here, we can learn much about teaching thinking by knowing *how* it is related to the subject matter. A plausible thesis, involving thinkers constucting semantic models, is outlined in Johnson-Laird (1988, Ch. 12) and substantiated and developed in Johnson-Laird (1991). If this thesis is right, then the way ahead is via content and semantics rather than the essentially abstract syntactic approach of traditional thinking models.

*Notes*

1. For many and varied examples see Schank, R. and Abelson, R.P. (1977), *Scripts, Plans, Goals and Understandings*, New Jersey, Lawrence Erlbaum.

2. For a general introduction and discussion of many of the examples in this paper see Garnham, A. (1987), *Artificial Intelligence*, London, Routledge.

*Bibliography*

Dreyfus, H.L. (1979), *What Computers Can't Do*, 2nd edition, New York, Harper and Row.

Gauld, A. and Shotter, J. (1977), *Human Action and its Psychological Investigation*, London, Routledge.

Johnson-Laird, P.N. (1988) *The Computer and the Mind* (Fontana Masterguides).

Johnson-Laird, P.N. and Byrne, R.M.J. (1991) *Deduction* (Hove, Erlbaum).

Lenat, D. (1982), 'The Nature of Heuristics', in *Artificial Intelligence*, Vol. 19.

Newell, A. and Simon, H.A. (1972), *Human Problem Solving*, New Jersey, Prentice Hall.

Wiezenbaum, J. (1976), *Computer Power and Human Reason*, San Francisco, W.H. Freeman.

Winston, P.H. (1977), *Artificial Intelligence*, Mass., Addison-Wesley.

# 4: 'LOGIC IN SCHOOLS': THE CARDIFF EXPERIMENT

## Humphrey Palmer

There was this student, hitch-hiking. People asked him what he was studying. Philosophy, he said; but then they would ask him what that was, and wonder why he found the question difficult. So he said 'I am a logician!' That silenced them. Some heard it as 'magician'. The others felt logic must be some sort of algebra, and changed the subject rapidly. (*The Times*)

That is how people think of Logic: mysterious, mathematical, boffinish, way out, and very specialised. Not at all the sort of thing that people do at school.

Logic nowadays is taught to Philosophy freshmen, plus a few Maths undergraduates: to about one student in thirty, or less than one half of one per cent of the population as a whole. So, are the others missing anything? That depends on what Logic has to offer them.

As a student of Logic you do come to distinguish between 'X follows' and 'X is true'; you learn to tell good arguments from bad, even in complicated instances; and you get to see how an argument can be disabled by another one which is clearly parallel and more plainly bad. You also practise 'analysis': working out what was really meant and re-expressing it. You may study how division and definition work. You will acquire a small technical vocabulary in which to refer to all these things. With all this you should gain the confidence to insist that nonsense is nonsense, and that *non sequiturs* do not prove anything.

Now most people are dealing in arguments on a daily basis, offering and receiving them and needing to assess their reliability. If a study of Logic helps with this then surely more people should be doing it.

### The Cardiff Project

From about 1972 these thoughts were troubling two Philosophy teachers in Cardiff. Both had seen what this study could do 'for those beset by arguments: persuasions open and hidden, put forward in books or on buses, blown up onto hoardings or piped right into the home by an illuminated box' (Evans and Palmer 1983). One had taught the subject in India, where it was still a popular option at Intermediate. Perhaps it could also help pupils at that stage over here, providing 'a plain man's form of self-defence, in a world much given to smear and bamboozle, to unproof and authoritative irrelevance' (Evans and Palmer 1983). After some hesitation we decided that the only way to find out was to try.

In 1974, with encouragement from our college and from Directors of Education, we put the idea to local secondary head-teachers. They suggested we provide an O-level course which could be taken in the lower-sixth. From 1975, a central class was held at the college one afternoon a week. Interested schools released their pupils for that afternoon, and were in due course informed which of them had come. Pupils paid their own bus fares and were free to withdraw. The class would begin with fifty or so and drop fairly quickly to twenty-five, who then mostly stayed the course. Some adults also came, pursuing valiantly. Cardiff and district had some twenty-seven secondary schools within a bus ride of the central class. Ten of these sent pupils to the class.

This class persuaded us that the subject could be taught to sixth-formers, and was of demonstrable use for any further study involving reasoning – and for life as well. We wrote our own booklets for the class, not finding any textbook suitable in content and in price. By this time Dr Meredydd Evans had joined the project, and he translated the booklets into Welsh for the Welsh-medium schools.

A central class, however, could never touch those beyond bus-reach. So the next step was to find and train some teachers for the subject. A few could remember doing it at college. Some saw that Logic was implicit in their training in Mathematics or in Science. Some were prepared to take the subject up from scratch. All needed a short course to enthuse and recall, and in 1980 this was provided, with Welsh Office help, to some twenty local teachers. Some of these then offered the subject in their schools, and the central class was dropped.

Over the next eight years the subject continued in these schools. We stood by for advice and encouragement, and spent some time looking for other teachers in schools further afield who might be interested in joining the project.

In 1982 the exam moved from Mode 2 (local option) to Mode 1, so that it was advertised throughout Wales. At the same time the syllabus was revised in the light of teachers' comments, including more on induction and on meaning and ambiguity.

In 1983 the text we had prepared as photocopied booklets was printed by the Extra-Mural Department of the University; when this edition sold out it was republished by the University of Wales Press in 1986. Some work was also done at this time preparing interactive self-teaching programmes for the BBC microcomputer, to help with solitary or distance learners.

The subject now seemed well established and ready to take off around Wales and across the border in England. Instead the schools originally teaching Logic around Cardiff gradually dropped from the project one by one and no new schools took it on. In some cases the teacher concerned was promoted or moved to another school. In others the extra work involved in introducing the GCSE left no spare time or energy for Logic. And of course O-level itself was to disappear. A GCSE replacement with assessed course work would mean an extra load on the teacher.

The last O-level examination was in 1988; by then some three hundred pupils had taken the subject. This meant the end of the Cardiff experiment in its original form. Of the three original promoters, one had by now retired to west Wales and folk song; another had moved to medical ethics, in Swansea; the third was head of another department in Cardiff. None was able to promote Logic all over again. What we had by then learnt, however, may be of interest.

### Content and technique

We had to decide early on just which logical topics we would teach; a matter made more difficult by an unnecessary and often uncivil war between followers of Russell and those of Aristotle! The 'traditional' logic seemed more accessible, being expressed at first in words, and then with initial letters written down 'for short'. The modern symbolic approach was more inclusive and more rigorous. We decided we should tackle both. At this level the main difference between the systems is one of convention: should 'All mermaids use combs' be taken as saying that mermaids really do exist, as well as combs? Adapting the theory of the syllogism to take the answer 'No' does not unsettle very much, and it is well for pupils to realise that even in Logic some differences are just conventional.

In teaching we soon came across what we call 'symbolfright': pupils arrive very wary of anything resembling algebra, some positively terrified. An unfamiliar symbol seems dangerous and magical, *mysterium tremendum et fascinans*. This reaction hinders many from learning Logic – or Mathematics, or Chemistry, or Greek. But this response can be modified if the symbols are introduced gradually, and are then handled and passed around. For the syllogism, we developed a variant of Lewis Carroll's diagram. Our version has two axes and a ring around the centre: areas are declared Occupied by a spot (or a coin), Vacant by a bar (toothpick or match). The match may then have to shove the coin from one area to another, as required by the argument ('matchpenny arguments', Evans and Palmer 1983, pp. 126 f.)

For propositional calculus a card game was developed, along the lines of *Lexicon*, with one logical constant or variable on each card. The players spell out allowable logical formulae (well-formed formulae) or add others Scrabblewise, or as following from those already put down. This helps in mastering the rules; the players teach and amuse each other instead of labouring solo on repetitive exercises. It also helps one get the hang of tautology and contradiction, and can even lead to the discovery of an unexpected rule or inference (Evans 1980, pp. 443-51).

*Whom should we teach?*
Children seem argumentative from an early age; so some may be receptive to the rules of right reasoning, say from the age of eight or ten. But we did not start there. We set out to teach Logic to sixth-formers, pupils only a year or two younger than those we already taught. Perhaps if some schoolteachers took the task on they would try it further down the school. One teacher in the project did take a fifth-form class successfully for several years. Maybe the association with O-level discouraged further experiment.

The class we taught was highly self-selected, and the O-level results were skewed accordingly. In the schools the subject was mainly taught as a special option, in some cases in the lunch hour. Logic itself is a truly *general* study, and we think some topics could come into a General Studies scheme if the modules are not too small. However, most of the topics are progressive (this week builds on last), and some answers to questions are actually wrong.

Where does the subject lead? It comes into some higher Mathematics. It would help those who need to know how a computer works. It is itself studied, with some puzzlement, in philosophical Logic. Not many will pursue it down these avenues. For most it just leads to better understanding and handling of arguments *on other subjects*. Now this enhanced understanding can be gained in one or two years' work.

*Getting the subject started*

You can't buy outsize shirts or tiny shoes because they are not what everybody wants. The same economic forces are now affecting schools, and all minority subjects are suffering – as are the pupils who would have studied them. Another current development is that everything a teacher does is being made contractual. Together these constraints look set to rule out all novelty and all development; after all, if people wanted their children to learn so-and-so they would be learning it already, wouldn't they?

These points apply to our project. It is a minority subject – must be, to begin with. Clearly we chose an odd time to start promoting it. It did depend on people doing something for nothing, with their own spare time and energy. We had the subject matter and the expertise, but not much acquaintance with educational machinery or fund-raising. No doubt we should have seen earlier that enthusiasm is not enough.

Tertiary and sixth-form colleges, it seems, are much freer to hire part-time teachers. With their varied intake these colleges will need some subjects which can be started there, subjects of a general character, preparing folk for life. So the move towards sixth-form colleges could be the salvation of Logic as a fairly general study. The wheel will have come full circle and brought us back to Intermediate by another name.

In this project we started out on one way of teaching reasoning skills; a traditional way, done late on at school, and leading to a public examination. Some others would favour starting much earlier. Some favour studying arguments directly, 'on the hoof', not dead and dissected in a standard textbook 'form' or diagram. All the various initiatives presented in this volume can, I believe, co-exist and help each other. For each will face the same problem: how to pick up participants.

As Logic or Reasoning has not been a regular and distinct item on the curriculum at school or, consequently, at teachers' colleges, few serving teachers have studied it. There is no ready-made network, no well-established subject association, to provide contacts and funds and channel enthusiasm. Initially those likely to respond are too few and far between for any one project to collect enough of them. We need some body which can trawl for them nation-wide, and put interested teachers in touch with some project to suit them and with other teachers near enough to be of help. To some extent, this trawling has begun through several national conferences, through the pages of *COGITO*, via the Thinking Skills Network, and by the present volume. It needs to go on more widely still.

*Bibliography*

Evans, D.M. (1980), 'Logicon: A Logic Game', in *Teaching Philosophy* 1980, pp. 443-541, reprinted in Wilson, A. (ed.) (1988), *Demonstrating Philosophy*, University Press of America.

Evans, D.M. and Palmer, H. (1983), *Understanding Arguments*, Department of Extra-Mural Studies, University College, Cardiff, reprinted by University of Wales Press/Drake Educational Associates, with cards and software. A Welsh version *Ymresymu i'r Newyddian* is available from the Department of Extra-Mural Studies, 38 Park Place, Cardiff CF1 3BB. Teachers can obtain a guide to the textbook from Logic in Schools, UW College, Cardiff CF1 3UW.

Palmer, H. (1980), 'Logic in Schools', *Mathematics Teacher*, June 1980, pp. 48-50.

*Logic-teaching programs for microcomputers*

*Why Study Arguments?*, for BBC-B; tape only; explains what logic is, and gets the user to do some; simple presentation; needs Microtext loaded in first; available on loan from Logic in Schools.

*Arguing for Beginners*, for BBC-B; tape or disc; similar content and style to *Why Study Arguments?* but needs no other program loaded in first; tape and disc for sale from Logic in Schools.

*Truth*, for BBC-B; exercises to go with textbook; checking program for well-formed formulae; displays check procedure; tape or disc with textbook: Newton-Smith, W. (1985), *Logic*, Oxford University Press.

*Prove*, for BBC-B; checking program for proofs in calculus of propositions; requires strict derivation; employs quantification; on same disc with *Truth* (above).

*John*, for IBM or Apple; disc; syllogistic reasoning via Venn diagrams; step by step self-tutor; colour and sound; available with booklet from Logical Products, Department of Philosophy, University of Hong Kong, Pokfulam Rd, H.K.

*Ludwig*, for IBM or Apple; truth-tables, tautology, contingency; available on separate disc from suppliers of *John*.

The following bulletins/newsletters contain lists of software designed to teach logic:

1. *The Computer and Philosophy Newsletter*, Centre for the Design of Educational Computing (Leslie Burkholder), Carnegie-Mello University, Pittsburgh, Penn 15213, USA.
2. *The Computerised Logic Teaching Bulletin*, Department of Logic and Metaphysics (Dr Stephen Reid), University of St Andrews, Fyfe, Scotland KY16 9AL.

The *Proceedings of a Conference on Programming for Logic Teaching*, University of Leeds, July 1987, Harry Lewis (ed.), is available from Computers in Teaching Initiative Support Service, University of Bath, Claverton Down, Bath BA2 7AY.

# 5: CRITICAL THINKING

## Alec Fisher

*A short story*
There was once a young, enthusiastic teacher, called Ernestine.
Ernestine enjoyed her subject, and she wanted to pass on her enthusiasm and knowledge to her pupils. However, she wanted more than
that. She also wanted to teach her pupils to *reason* well, to eschew bad
arguments and to value good ones, to be *clear-headed* and to *think for
themselves* in arriving at decisions about what to do and believe.
Ernestine wanted her pupils to learn these skills and values through
the way in which she taught her own subject, of course. However, she
also hoped that such skills and values would transfer to other domains.
    Ernestine was a 'good' teacher. Her students enjoyed their work,
they learned the 'standard' material thoroughly, and they were good
at reproducing it in examinations. However, she gradually came to
feel that her hopes were not being fully realised and that she was
failing to teach the *general and transferable thinking skills* which she
thought so important. She felt that pressures on her time encouraged
rote-learning of what she had said in class, and she had great difficulty
in finding books and teaching resources which helped her teach
thinking skills. As she discussed this with other people she discovered
that many of her colleagues shared her hopes and frustrations. Of
course, everyone agreed that school children should be taught to
think; indeed, most teachers asserted that they *were* teaching their
pupils to think. However, Ernestine found that few people agreed
about what this meant in detail or what it entailed. At the same time,
she *also* discovered that there were many experiments taking place in
teaching thinking skills and that experimental materials were available to help her. That was how Ernestine became involved in the
'critical thinking movement', which has grown so rapidly in recent
years throughout North America and which is the subject of this
chapter.

*The origins of the critical thinking movement*
Although teachers have been interested in teaching people to think
at least since Socrates, current concerns with critical thinking are

generally traced back to the work of the American philosopher, psychologist and educationalist, John Dewey. One of the first discussions of critical thinking – which Dewey called 'reflective thinking' – is to be found in his book *How We Think* (1909). The book is based on Dewey's work in the Chicago Laboratory School and much of it reflects conversations with teachers who were trying to implement his ideas. An important and striking feature of the book is the extent to which it is interdisciplinary – it draws on Philosophy, on Psychology and on teaching experience – and that is very characteristic of modern work on critical thinking.

The next major development in the critical thinking tradition was probably Edward Glaser's *An Experiment in the Development of Critical Thinking*, published in 1941. As a student at the Advanced School of Education at Teacher's College, Columbia University, Glaser designed an experiment into the teaching of critical thinking which was a model of scientific procedure. In short, he devised a range of teaching materials for the use of teachers in teaching critical thinking. The teachers were then briefed on the objectives of the experiment and on the basic concepts and methods involved (Glaser adopted Dewey's conception of critical thinking though he broke it into a number of specific abilities). After the teachers had each taught a ten week course in critical thinking, their students' critical thinking abilities were assessed and compared with the abilities of children in control groups who had had no special instruction.

The *Watson-Glaser Critical Thinking Appraisal* was developed as part of this study and, subsequently, revised versions of this test have been widely used to test critical thinking abilities. It is now probably the most widely used test of critical thinking abilities in the world (despite its manifest weaknesses).

Though it seems unlikely to us now that a ten week course could have any lasting effect on critical thinking abilities, Glaser's pioneering study is of considerable historical importance in the development of the critical thinking tradition.

In 1962 the *Harvard Educational Review* published an article by Robert Ennis which is still rightly regarded as a landmark in this field. The article was called 'A Concept of Critical Thinking: A Proposed Basis for Research in the Teaching and Evaluation of Critical Thinking Ability', and its objective was to detail what critical thinking means and entails.

In this article, Ennis lists what he calls 'twelve aspects of critical thinking' and 'three dimensions'. In short, the focus is on grasping the *meaning* of a statement, avoiding *ambiguity*, spotting *contradictions*, judging what *follows*, what is *assumed* and when a conclusion is *warranted*, deciding when a *definition* is adequate, when an *observation statement* or *authority* are reliable, and deciding when a problem has been properly *identified* and adequately resolved.

Ennis then presents a detailed discussion of each of the elements he has identified, which is intended to be sufficient for teaching and evaluation purposes. The paper is still well worth reading.

Much of this early work was conducted in relative isolation. However, the past two decades have seen a rapid growth in what has become known as the Informal Logic and Critical Thinking movement. This is not so much a 'movement' as a large number of related experiments. These experiments differ in many ways, but they all share a similar objective: to improve reasoning skills and critical thinking skills by *direct* methods, i.e. methods designed specifically for that purpose. In part, these experiments have arisen as a reaction against the belief that reasoning skills are best taught *indirectly*, i.e. by teaching some other *subject* such as elementary formal Logic, Classics, History or Mathematics. The problem with this approach is, in short, that *transfer* simply does not occur. In part, these experiments have arisen as a reaction against the belief that all reasoning is subject-specific; on which view the only way to learn to reason well in a given field is to master the subject matter of that field, whether it be History, Physics, Medicine or whatever. (For a forceful exposition of this view see John McPeck's *Critical Thinking and Education*, which is discussed below.) In short, this view claims too much; an *ad hominem* fallacy is a fallacy in any field; more generally, there are principles of reasoning which apply in many fields. However, the main drive behind these various experiments appears to be an increasing demand for general reasoning skills and a widespread conviction that clear and logical thinking ought to be teachable.

## Some current programmes

In this section we briefly explain three current approaches to teaching critical thinking, which belong in the informal logic and critical thinking tradition.

**Informal Logic** courses are mostly aimed at the college and university level. In these, students are taught at the very least how to identify the conclusions, reasons and structure of a piece of reasoning. This is usually done by using linguistic clues. Students are then given some general criteria for distinguishing good and bad arguments; these sometimes include some standard propositional logic, some classic fallacies and the deductive-inductive distinction. The key point is that the method concentrates on real arguments, taken from sources ranging from newspapers to classic texts, rather than on the usual, invented ones, familiar to formal logicians. Michael Scriven's book *Reasoning* (1976) set the agenda for this kind of approach. One of the most widely used textbooks in this tradition is Trudy Govier's *A Practical Study of Argument* (1985).

**The Philosophy for Children Programme** is the subject of specific attention in Chapter 7 of the present book. The programme's author is former Professor of Philosophy at Columbia University, Matthew Lipman. His explicit objective was to teach children to *think* for themselves instead of learning by rote and simply accepting the authority of their teachers. It is easy to have this laudable aim, but it is much harder to devise a curriculum which will realise it. The vehicle Lipman chose was appropriately adapted philosophical discussion. His main interest is in developing reasoning skills so that children can:

> draw sound inferences, offer convincing reasons, flush out underlying assumptions, establish defensible classifications and definitions, organise coherent explanations, descriptions and arguments. (Lipman 1985, p. 18)

He can now cite good empirical evidence that his programme is successful and that children taught reasoning through Philosophy have shown marked improvement in reasoning skills. (See Lipman and Gazzard, 'Philosophy for Children: Where We Are Now'.)

**'Strong' Critical Thinking.** In another experiment, students are not only taught the 'micro-skills' of the informal logician, but they are also taught (where appropriate) to locate arguments in a broader cultural context, to recognise their personal prejudices and the prejudices of their society; and they are shown how to evaluate arguments in this broader context. The leading exponent of this approach is Professor Richard Paul, Director of the Center for Critical Thinking and Moral Critique at Sonoma State University, California. As he puts it in a forthcoming paper, 'Critical Thinking and the Critical Person':

> Much that we learn...is distinctly irrational. [We] come to believe any number of things without knowing how or why...[We] believe for irrational reasons: because those around us believe, because we are rewarded for believing, because we are afraid to disbelieve, because our vested interest is served by belief...In all these cases our beliefs are without rational grounding...we become rational on the other hand, to the extent that our beliefs and actions are grounded in good reasons and evidence...to the extent we have cultivated a passion for clarity, accuracy and fairmindedness. These global skills, passions and dispositions, integrated with a way of acting and thinking, are what characterise the rational, the educated and, in my sense, the critical person.

Another source of materials for those who wish to experiment with teaching critical thinking is to be found in a series of books, by Professor Paul and collaborators, which are in the process of being published. The main purpose of each book is to help school teachers to remodel their existing lessons so that they teach critical thinking skills (in short, exactly what Ernestine was looking for). The first book in the series is called *Critical Thinking Handbook K-3: A Guide For Remodelling Lesson Plans in Language, Arts, Social Studies and Science*. It is aimed at those teaching children in the range kindergarten to grade 3 (children aged 5 to 8); the second is for grades 4-6 (children aged 9 to 11). In what follows we shall refer to the first book as *K-3* and the second as *4-6*. [Since this chapter was first published, two further volumes have been published, one for grades 6-9 and one for High School: for full details see bibliography. – eds]

Each book is self-contained and each has the same form. First there is a general account of what critical thinking is, and then there is an explanatory list of 'strategies' for teaching critical thinking (28 strategies in *K-3*; 31 in *4-6*). However, most of the book comprises lesson plans in their original and remodelled forms. The originals are criticised in the light of the principles of critical thinking, and the reasons for the remodelled plans are explained in terms of the strategies for teaching critical thinking (58 lessons in *K-3*; 40 in *4-6*).

Two brief examples, from *K-3*, will give the flavour. In the first (p. 183) the issue is whether air has weight. In the original lesson plan, children learn that air has weight by doing two experiments. In one they balance two full balloons on a yard-stick and then let the air out of one of the balloons. In the other experiment they compare the weight of a basketball when it is empty and when it is full of air.

In the revised lesson plan, the teacher begins with the question, 'Does air weigh anything?' and allows discussion. The next question is, 'How could we find out?' Here, the objective is to 'foster independent thinking' (strategy 1). The children may need to be led to think of the experiments just mentioned or something similar, but the intention is to get the children to do as much as possible themselves. When they have done the experiments (or any others they thought of) they are asked, 'What did you observe? What did you conclude? How did the experiment settle the issue?', and the objective is to get the children to explain their reasoning as fully as possible (strategy 18) and to make them 'comfortable' about doing this and being expected to do it. Part of this process requires them to make their assumptions explicit (strategy 14), and the teacher encourages this with suitable questioning.

Paul is best known for his distinction between 'weak' and 'strong' critical thinking. Briefly, the weak critical thinker is skilled in the techniques of argument, but uses these skills only to pursue his or her own narrow selfish interests. The strong critical thinker is skilled in the techniques of argument, and uses them 'fairmindedly'. Fairminded critical thinkers not only subject the views of other people and other societies (having interests and ideologies different from their own) to critical scrutiny, but they are just as ready to subject their own interests, preferences, prejudices and ideologies to critical scrutiny.

A very brief second example from *K-3* should illustrate the idea. In this lesson the children read a story. In the story Eddie collects things that he calls 'valuable property', but which his father calls 'junk'. One day Eddie buys two things from an antique shop. At first his father is angry, but then he decides he wants one of the things and he buys it from Eddie. Eddie's mother buys the other. Eddie's father is proud of the profit Eddie made and suggests they go into business together 'selling junk'.

In the original lesson plan, pupils are asked to do the following things: recall story details; guess Eddie's mother's attitudes; list objects found in antique shops; make and justify inferences; describe the difference between junk and antiques; calculate Eddie's profit; and select a sentence which expresses the main idea of the story.

In his critique of this lesson plan Paul says:

> This story describes a clash of two perspectives. The disagreement between Eddie and his father provides an excellent model for many conflicts. It includes a specific issue (i.e. 'Does Eddie collect junk or valuable property?'); two sets of incompatible concepts applied to the same phenomena; and two lines of reasoning based on contradictory evaluative assumptions (i.e. objects which look interesting or appealing are valuable; only those objects which can be used or sold for profit are valuable). Yet the suggested questions fail to take advantage of the story. (*K-3*, p. 83)

In the remodelled lesson plan, children are asked to *identify key concepts* themselves – rather than being told them – thus *fostering independent thinking* (strategy 1). They are asked to *clarify these concepts* with examples (strategy 12), and to say what is *implied* by calling something 'junk' etc. (strategy 21). They are asked to *identify the assumptions held* by Eddie and his father, including their different values (strategy 14), and to try to *see things from both perspectives* (strategy 3). They are asked to carefully note the facts in the case, to distinguish those which are *relevant* from those which are *irrelevant* to the argument (strategy 16) and to distinguish the facts from what they (the pupils) *infer* from them (strategy 17). They are also asked to say what changed through the story: 'Was it assumptions, use of terms, values, or what?' They may also engage in dialogue and role-playing, etc.

The emphasis throughout is on getting children to think for themselves. The objective is that they should be clear-headed and should reason things through for themselves, especially by considering alternative perspectives, *and that they should value doing this*. The method employed by the teacher is essentially that of Socratic questioning and dialogue: 'What does this *mean*? What is Eddie *assuming*? What is *implied*?' etc.

Again, though Paul's books are written for North American children, so that the examples do not always readily transfer to the British context, this too is an experiment from which we can learn.

### John McPeck's challenge

The most notable and systematic critique of the critical thinking tradition whose emergence we have been describing, is to be found in John McPeck's book, *Critical Thinking and Education*. His position is clearly expressed in the following paragraph:

> [critical thinking] is the appropriate use of *reflective scepticism* within the problem area under consideration, and knowing how and when to apply this reflective scepticism effectively requires, among other things, knowing something about the field in question. Thus we may say of someone that he is a critical thinker about X if he has the propensity and skill to engage in X (be it mathematics, politics or mountain climbing) with reflective scepticism. There is, moreover, no reason to believe that a person who thinks critically in one area will be able to do so in another. The transfer of training skills cannot be assumed of critical thinking but must be established in each case by means of empirical tests. Calling to witness such notorious cases as distinguished logicians with no idea for whom to vote, nor why, it is fair to postulate that no one can think critically about everything, as there are no Renaissance men in this age of specialised knowledge. (p. 7)

In short, McPeck's view is that critical thinking is *subject-specific*, that what *counts* as critical thinking differs from subject to subject, that there are no *general* skills which can be applied in all fields, and that therefore there is no reason to expect *transfer* of critical thinking skills from one domain to another (i.e. one could be a critical thinker in one field without being anything of the sort in others).

McPeck's criticisms have generated strong reactions from those working in the field but they remain important and well worth reading.

## In conclusion

Largely as a result of his pioneering and subsequent work in the field, Robert Ennis' definition of critical thinking has gained wide acceptance in recent years. It neatly articulates some of the central ideas at the heart of the tradition we have just been describing.

> Critical thinking is reasonable, reflective thinking that is focussed on deciding what to believe or do. (Ennis and Norris 1989, p. 1)

This definition extends previous ones due to Dewey, Glazer and Ennis (which spoke only of reasoning about *beliefs*) by explicitly including reasoning about *actions*, and this is obviously right given the practical importance critical thinking is supposed to have in our everyday lives.

It is common nowadays to stress that teachers are not only interested in teaching critical thinking *abilities*. They want their students to have the *disposition* to use those abilities, and to *value* their use in deciding what to do and believe.

We should perhaps note at this point that many working in this field are, or have been, unhappy with the term 'critical thinking' because of its negative connotations. In his paper 'Rational Thinking and Educational Practice' Ennis used the term 'rational thinking', but established usage in North America has forced him to revert to 'critical thinking'. In the UK we could use 'reflective thinking', 'rational thinking', 'critical thinking' or perhaps even 'logical thinking' – all of these terms capture something of what we are interested in.

The growth in informal logic and critical thinking in North America has been very marked during the past decade. Many schools, colleges and universities now teach courses of this general kind. For example, in 1982 the California State University system adopted a requirement that all their 300,000 students receive training in critical thinking so that they would have:

> an understanding of the relationship of language to logic, leading to the ability to analyse, criticise and advocate ideas, to reason inductively and deductively, and to reach factual or judgemental conclusion, based on sound inferences drawn from unambiguous statements of knowledge or belief. (See Paul 1985, p. 2)

Many other institutions have now adopted similar objectives; these are mainly, but not exclusively, in the USA and Canada. There are also many texts now available which provide different approaches to teaching informal logic and critical thinking skills, though so far nearly all of these are North American.

It is to be hoped that more of these initiatives and experiments in teaching thinking skills will become more widely known in the UK.

*Bibliography*

Dewey, J. (1909), *How We Think*, D.C. Heath & Co.

Ennis, R.H. (1962), 'A Concept of Critical Thinking', *Harvard Educational Review* Vol. 32, No. 1, pp. 81-111.

Ennis, R.H. and Norris, S. (1990) *Evaluating Critical Thinking*, Midwest, CA.

Ennis, R.H. (1981), 'Rational Thinking and Educational Practice', in Soltis, J. (ed.), *Philosophy and Education*, Volume I of the eightieth yearbook of the National Society for the Study of Education, Chicago, NSSE.

Fisher, A.E. (ed.) (1988), *Critical Thinking: Proceedings of the First British Conference on Informal Logic and Critical Thinking*, University of East Anglia.

Glaser, E. (1941), *An Experiment in the Development of Critical Thinking*, Teachers College, Colombia University, New York.

Govier, T. (1985), *A Practical Study of Argument*, Wadsworth Publishing Co.

Lipman, M. (1974), *Harry Stottlemeier's Discovery*, Institute for the Advancement of Philosophy for Children.

Lipman, M. (1976), *Lisa*, Institute for the Advancement of Philosophy for Children.

Lipman, M. and Gazzard, A., 'Philosophy for Children: Where We Are Now', in *Thinking*, Vol. 6, No. 4, pp. S1-S12.

Lipman, M. (1985), 'Philosophy for Children and Critical Thinking', in *National Forum*, Winter 1985, pp. 18-21.

McPeck, J. (1981), *Critical Thinking and Education*, Robertson.

Paul, R., Binker, A.J.A. and Charbonneau, M. (1986), *Critical Thinking Handbook K-3*, Center for Critical Thinking, Sonoma State University, California.

Paul, R., Binker, A.J.A., Jensen, K. and Kreklau, H. (1987), *Critical Thinking Handbook 4-6*, Center for Critical Thinking, Sonoma State University, California.

Paul, R. (1985), 'The Critical Thinking Movement', in *National Forum*, Winter 1985, pp. 2-3.

Paul, Richard W., *et al.*, *Critical Thinking Handbook: 6th-9th. A Guide to remodelling Lesson Plans in Language Arts, Social Studies, and Sciences*, Center for Critical Thinking, Sonoma State University, California.

Paul, Richard W., *et al.*, *Critical Thinking Handbook: High School. A Guide for Redesigning Instruction*, Center for Critical Thinking, Sonoma State University, California.

Paul, Richard W., *Critical Thinking: What Every Person Needs to Survive in a Rapidly Changing World*, A.J.A. Binker (ed.), Center for Critical Thinking, Sonoma State University, California.

Scriven, M. (1976), *Reasoning*, McGraw-Hill.

# 6: PHILOSOPHY IN THE SIXTH FORM

## Dermot O'Keeffe

The sixth form has traditionally been regarded as a reasonable context for philosophical initiation. In many schools, perhaps especially in the private sector, students have long been exposed to philosophical theories, characters and texts in Liberal Studies, Humanities or Oxbridge classes. They are expected to have the ability to deal with primary sources by, say, Descartes or Plato, and to evaluate different viewpoints and sustain philosophical enquiries or arguments. This expectation is undoubtedly nourished partly by the knowledge that the Higher Education entrance process – whether oral or written – may well demand a critical capacity not directly related to the student's A-levels.

It is a reasonable expectation for other and better reasons, however. At 16 +, and after the wide ranging and hectic business of GCSEs, the student may well have a strong natural desire to stand back and ask questions which concern 'everything in general and nothing in particular'. It may seem appropriate to ask: What is History (or Science, or Art, or Education)?, where these questions concern the *nature* of these concepts, and cannot be answered ostensively, merely by reference to a shelf in the library.

In a period devoted to aporetic enquiry, the questions will multiply: What is goodness? What is the self? What is the purpose of the state? What is certain? The questions may well become more reflexive, amusing and demanding. Is this question fair? Could God make a bowl of porridge bigger than he could eat? Could you have been someone else? Why?

The sixth form is ideally a liberation after the content-heavy fifth year. It is suddenly legitimate to be subversive or pedantic. Finding things difficult is suddenly a virtue, not a fault, provided the difficulty originates in the appreciation of a problem's complexity. The identification of ambiguities, and the corresponding repertoire of distinctions, mean that *reading* – a process once so simple – becomes hard work which demands insight and creativity. The esoteric and exclusive aspects of Philosophy are obviously attractive. The comfortable, pre-reflective worldview is exchanged for an uncomfortable, problem-ridden one. The philosopher's interlocutor is set to work and forced to explain himself; discussions range less widely but more deeply. Common sense does not necessarily hold pride of place, and may appear as little more than a flimsy and dogmatic metaphysic. Everything is fair game, and this period is often characterised by a sense of urgency, an almost daily adjustment of viewpoint and an attitude of creative subversion.

Moreover, with the right support, questions which may otherwise have been dismissed as intractable may now be entertained and refined. The Big Questions may be respectable after all: students are young enough to ask *fundamental* questions, and not yet old enough to have given up hope that such enquiries might prove worthwhile. In this sense Philosophy is, like Mozart, 'too easy for children and too difficult for adults'. The sixth form is, or can be, a useful incubation for philosophical neonates. Another reason why Philosophy should be pursued in the sixth form is that it creates a logical space for a new discipline within the horizons of the student. In a society in which libraries stock philosophical works alongside books on UFOs and the occult, Philosophy in the curriculum effectively provides students with another option to consider with regard to higher education.

Philosophy also provides a common ground for both Science and Humanities students, and combines literary and linguistic skills with technical and logical ones.

There is a debate about whether or not analytical skills, developed in Philosophy, transfer to other subjects. It seems a shame that other disciplines do not actually contain philosophical options or modules, where appropriate, because if the suspected lack of transfer involved *content* it would presumably be thereby corrected. The failure to develop and transfer more specifically *logical* skills may concern a difference between logical and psychological models of thought (Morton 1988).

Perhaps, in practice, logical thinking can be developed along the same lines as good grammar – principally by exposure to good practice. To intuitively know that a sentence is ungrammatical, but not know exactly how or why (in syntactical terms), may not be ideal, but it is better than not knowing there is *anything* wrong with it. Technical and diagnostic skills can be developed along the way; Philosophy is, after all, 'like trying to build a raft on the high seas'.

In any case, the majority of discussions seem to concern the meaning, justification, truth and implication of particular premises, and the coherence and consistency of terms, far more than they concern validity as exemplified in logic textbooks. Provided the teacher is sensitive to the issue of validity, and capable of raising questions and supplying counter examples (a technique which certainly *is* transferable), there is no reason why detailed and substantive disputes cannot take place.

Another difficulty with the teaching of 'microskills', which seeks to analyse and illuminate densely written passages, is that such enquiries are prone to be too particular or localised, or even simply superficial. The context is not simply an optional extra but a prerequisite to the understanding of a piece of reasoning. Commenting on such views, propounded by Professor Richard Paul, Professor Trudi Govier writes:

> Paul's view is that the analysis of arguments, as typically pursued by informal logicians...is done on far too small a scale. People handle arguments atomistically. Then take them out of context, removing key claims identified as premises and conclusions from a rich socio-political scene...Atomistic argument analysis will give only 'weak' critical thinking because it does not force us to look at the broader background from which the argument itself and our attitude towards it have emerged...For genuine, or 'strong' critical thinking to occur, students have to identify the conceptual framework or worldviews presumed in...arguments and in themselves, and they have to have the ability and the disposition to critically evaluate them. (Govier, in Fisher 1988, p. 7)

Govier goes on to criticise 'strong' critical thinking for being, basically, over-ambitious. However, Paul's hermeneutical point should surely be relevant in the sixth form, especially in a culture where analytical philosophers have traditionally regarded their work as an essentially pure and ahistorical method of conceptional analysis. The development of 'strong' critical thinking could form a useful counterpoint to the prevailing stance, so well described by Alasdair MacIntyre:

> We all often still treat the moral philosophers of the past as contributors to a single debate with a relatively unvarying subject-matter, treating Plato and Hume and Mill as contemporaries both of ourselves and of each other. This leads to an abstraction of these writers from the cultural and social milieus in which they lived and thought and so the history of their thought acquires a false independence from the rest of the culture. Kant ceases to be part of the history of Prussia, Hume is no longer a Scotsman. For from the standpoint of moral philosophy as we conceive it these characteristics have become irrelevances. (MacIntyre 1981, p. 11)

A similar criticism of an exclusively analytical approach may be levelled from the standpoint of speech-act theory. On this view, the meaning of a proposition is not exhausted by 'sense and reference' considerations alone, but requires considerations of context ('the complete speech act'), just as much. For example, *in vacuo* 'Edinburgh is a very prosperous city', means one thing; in the context of Prime Minister's question-time it means quite another (roughly: 'I agree; the Chancellor's in serious trouble!').

Although the employment of the broader hermeneutical approach would be very demanding on both students and teachers, it should perhaps be recognised as a valuable and desirable contribution to critical thinking.

At the COGITO 1988 Conference at Bristol University, the subject of appraisal was raised, and proved very difficult. There seems to be a marked difference of opinion among sixth form teachers about what actually constitutes a good Philosophy essay, and a few years ago a disagreement among AEB examiners led to a heated exchange in the *Times Educational Supplement*, which called into question the whole idea of assessing A-level Philosophy. Some teachers think an oral examination would be a positive addition to the present system; others believe that stepped questions about a fresh argument would help. In any case, the Philosophy A-levels are an important development, and it is to the matter of their content that I now turn.

The AEB and JMB Philosophy A-levels differ in both form and content.

The JMB syllabus contains a 'core' comprising of Epistemology (selections from Plato's *Republic*, Descartes' *Meditations* and Hume's *Enquiry Concerning Human Understanding*) and Moral Philosophy (selections from Plato's *Republic*, Aristotle's *Ethics*, Mill's *Utilitarianism* and Nietzsche's *Beyond Good and Evil*).

It also contains three options (again based upon prescribed texts) in Philosophy of Mind, Philosophy of Religion and Political Philosophy.

There is also a JMB A/S-level based upon the 'core' of the A-level.

The AEB syllabus does not contain a compulsory 'core', but offers a choice of four historical periods (of which two must be studied) for the textual part of the course. These are:

1. Selections from Plato's *Republic* and *Gorgias*, and Aristotle's *Ethics*.

2. Selections from Descartes' *Meditations* and Hume's *Enquiry*.

3. Selections from Marx and Engels' *The German Ideology* and, in its entirety, Mill's *On Liberty*.

4. Russell's *The Problems of Philosophy,* Sartre's *Existentialism and Humanism* and Ayer's *Language, Truth and Logic*.

It also includes a choice of three from six themes, which do not involve prescribed texts, but a general reading list. The six themes are:

1. Scepticism.
2. Faith and the Existence of God.
3. Mind and Body.
4. Scientific Method.
5. Value Judgements.
6. Freedom, Law and Authority.

The AEB syllabus has greater flexibility than that of the JMB and is not so directly tied to specific texts; this probably means that the thematic is both more demanding and potentially more rewarding. Also the themes may be chosen to complement the historical texts, in order to enhance either the depth (where they overlap) or breadth (where they do not) of the course. The AEB option 'Value Judgements' is something of a misnomer because it concerns only ethics and not aesthetics or axiology generally.

Both syllabuses allow for interesting combinations with other A-levels. English Language and Theatre Studies, in my experience, are fruitful partnerships, and so are Art and Natural Science, depending upon the commitment of the student.

The strong points of Philosophy at A-level must be that it is pitched about right and is genuinely representative of the sort of thing a Philosophy undergraduate might encounter. If the numbers of students opting for Philosophy are big enough, the course can have a marked effect upon the ethos of the sixth form, and, in particular, debating and discussing generally are improved.

The aims and objectives of both JMB and AEB are, unsurprisingly, very similar. What remains unstated, but the teacher presumably assumes, is that a disposition to employ the various thinking skills should be developed. Fluency in Philosophy, like fluency in a second language, is surely about thinking in a different way entirely, rather than making passable responses. Philosophy A-level is baptism by total immersion, and the students who benefit most are undoubtedly those who have the confidence to concentrate upon skills, techniques and distinction rather than those who have an acquisitive attitude, and frantically build up a repertoire of set arguments for and against various theories. I am not at all convinced that the examination system has the capacity to distinguish between these two approaches, though distinguish it should. (This criticism applies, of course, to a variety of examination subjects.)

It is as encouraging to see the beneficial effects of Philosophy upon the committed student as it is chastening to see the absence of any such effects upon the acquisitive, content-crazed student. The fact that Philosophy is not, and need not be, simply a 'bolt on' extra, but can transform the way one listens, reads and argues, is one of the most attractive aspects of the subject. Perhaps the exam boards could devise a method – more skills-based and less content-bound – which would distinguish between the student who has appropriated critical techniques and the student who has rehearsed, passively, appropriate responses.

Another philosophical skill, and a creative one which often goes unrewarded, is a certain type of puzzlement; the ability to recognise a problem and ask – even if one cannot begin to answer – a range of questions which identify an area worth working on. A gifted student can produce a list of questions and problems simply by considering, say, the relation of reason and emotion, or the author's intention and a text's meaning. Simply fixing the co-ordinates of a problem is a demanding job, and certainly a good starting-point for some brain-storming.

Philosophy as a non-examination subject has a very strong rationale in the sixth form, and two areas – both of which form options on both A-level courses – have a particularly good case. Philosophy of Mind is interesting and involves distinctions (type/token, sense/reference, substance/attribute, etc.) which are useful and helpful vis-à-vis the subject generally. It is also adjacent to other areas, such as Psycho-analysis and Cognitive Science, which deserve attention and could enhance curriculum development. Political Philosophy, both historically and thematically, is self-evidently highly appropriate to sixth form work, and it is something of a scandal, in my view, that it is not more prevalent. With TVEI projects and the emergence of Economic Awareness, Political Philosophy has the opportunity to make itself known to a wider public. It will certainly be interesting to see if it develops into a critical 'interlocutor' to run alongside such initiatives.

Here at The Trinity School, Leamington Spa, in 1986 the SCDC funded an interdepartmental study (Philosophy and Theatre Studies) on Bioethics, when an opportunity was taken to examine medical possibilities from emotional and rational perspectives. Work in progress at present includes a project on personal identity from both philosophical and literary (Beckett, Kafka, Pirandello) points of view.

Possibilities of interdepartmental work and curriculum development are plentiful. It is up to Philosophy students and teachers to realise them.

*Bibliography*

Fisher, A. (ed.) (1988), *Critical Thinking: Proceedings of the First British Conference on Informal Logic and Critical Thinking*, University of East Anglia.

Govier, T., 'Ways of Teaching Reasoning Directly', in Fisher (1988).

MacIntyre, A. (1981), *After Virtue*, Notre Dame.

Martin, A., 'Making Arguments Explicit: The Theoretical Interest of Practical Difficulties', in Fisher (1988).

# 7:  PHILOSOPHY FOR CHILDREN

## M.J.Whalley

*Origins and aims*

In the early 1970s, Matthew Lipman, then Professor of Philosophy at Columbia University, New York, became concerned at the fact that students entering the university to take Philosophy courses were deficient in elementary reasoning ability. Their otherwise successful progress through the school system had not enabled them to think logically.

Now Philosophy is the one subject which examines reasoning in general, in all its various manifestations. This suggested the idea of introducing Philosophy into the school curriculum. In 1974 Lipman published the first edition of *Harry Stottlemeier's Discovery*, a long story (seventeen chapters) for ten to twelve year olds, designed to introduce philosophical topics, including some elementary logic. It was planned to use this for initiating discussion in the classroom, thus helping to sharpen pupils' skill in reasoning.

It quickly became apparent however that a story built around philosophical topics was not in itself adequate to enable most teachers to initiate philosophical discussion. Together with colleagues from the fields of Education and Philosophy therefore, Lipman developed extensive back-up material to be used in conjunction with the story. This was eventually put together as a teachers' manual (*Philosophical Inquiry*).The two main features of the manual are some notes for teachers relating to the main topics in each chapter of the story, and a large number of exercises designed to aid discussion of those topics.

In 1974 the Institute for the Advancement of Philosophy for Children (IAPC) was founded, and based at Montclair State College in New Jersey. Its aims were to develop further curriculum materials along similar lines, and to set up procedures for training teachers in their use, for it was soon found that even the provision of teaching manuals in no way guaranteed that teachers would be able to use them to achieve the desired end. This important aspect of 'Philosophy for Children' – its insistence upon a certain methodological approach in the classroom – will be taken up later, after a consideration of the materials currently available.

The book already referred to, *Harry Stottlemeier's Discovery*, took reasoning as its central theme, developing traditional (Aristotelian) logic to the point of looking at one simple form of the syllogism, and also dealing in an introductory way with types of informal logic and some fallacies. If this makes it seem rather textbook-like, it should be pointed out that this logical theme is presented in the fictional context of children posing questions about reasoning and attempting to answer them for themselves. In addition, several of the chapters raise issues taken from some of the main areas of philosophical inquiry, such as the Philosophy of Science, Ethics, Metaphysics, and Epistemology.

From this starting point, other books were written as sequels, using the same characters, and each concentrating on a particular area of inquiry. Thus *Lisa*, aimed at about the thirteen to fourteen year old age group, deals centrally with ethical issues; *Suki* looks at the problems of aesthetics, with special attention to writing poetry and prose; *Mark* is concerned with Social and Political Philosophy. These latter two are aimed more towards the upper end of secondary school. Each of these books has its own teaching manual, analogous to the one described for *Harry*. The concentration on a particular area of philosophy is a matter of emphasis only. The pursuit of almost any philosophical problem may raise questions related to other branches of the subject; so we should not be surprised to find in *Suki*, for example, Harry discussing with his father problems that seem to have more to do with the Philosophy of Science or Epistemology than Aesthetics. Harry's writing assignment has led him to explore the relation between writing and observation – but observation is linked to perception which leads him to question what exactly is perceived.

The next stage in the development of the IAPC curriculum was the development of materials for earlier age groups. For seven to nine year olds there are two titles: *Pixie* and *Kio and Gus*, again with their corresponding manuals. A fundamental theme of the former is the notion of a relationship. In *Harry*, some attention had been paid to the logical implications of sentences expressing simple relations, such as 'Jill is taller than Laura', but the nature of the relationship was not discussed. In *Pixie*, this question is approached from two directions: by looking at metaphysical problems concerning the nature of space and time; and by examining the use of metaphors and similes (among other things), which can be seen to depend on relationships. To mention such abstruse topics in the context of young school children's education may seem mind-boggling. But the important point is that children of seven or eight use language in a very sophisticated way; what they are rarely called on to do at school is *reflect* upon that usage.

The ability to use concepts implies the ability to distinguish one thing from another. If this can be done it is possible to compare one thing with another – to look for similarities and differences. These basic notions lie behind the metaphorical use of language.

As a result of these explorations, the context of *Pixie* and of *Kio and Gus* is only partly philosophical, and the manuals include in addition numerous exercises dealing with various ways that relationships are expressed in sentences. In *Pixie*, the metaphysical issues are easily raised by the main character herself, who is curious about most things, such as the relation of herself to her body, how a male cat can be a mammal when it does not suckle its young, whether 'space' and 'time' are merely words, and even why her older sister Miranda does not appear to wonder about any of these things. Stylistically, an important factor making for the success of *Pixie* with children is its sense of humour.

The underlying idea of similarities and differences can be applied also to wondering about the natural world. This is the main theme of *Kio and Gus*, with its focus on animals in particular. Just as in aesthetics, problems to do with perception come into play when we consider how we observe events and things. These are given a special slant in *Kio and Gus* by the fact that one of the main characters is blind.

Finally, the most recent addition to the IAPC curriculum is *Elfie*, designed for the first two years of school. The title of its teaching manual is *Getting Our Thoughts Together*. In it, interesting use is made of nursery rhymes to dish up further food for thought.

Lipman's decision to embed the teaching of reasoning within the discipline of Philosophy is a vitally important one. I have argued the case for Philosophy in schools elsewhere (Whalley 1987), and will here simply note a few of the main points.

1. Doing Philosophy entails engaging in dialogue, where reasons are offered in support of opinions; reasons which are in turn open to examination by those wishing to support contrary opinions.

2. To aid this process philosophers have over the centuries examined by what criteria one statement can be said to support another, and have thus developed the study of formal and informal logic.

3. The fundamental urge that gives rise to Philosophy – curiosity about the world at large and our relation to it – is shared by children. Young children have a natural bent for the subject because they wonder about things and want to question assumptions.

4. Lipman's curriculum taps into this usually thwarted urge for philosophical exploration, allowing children the chance to learn to reason by actually doing it in the process of discussing issues of

interest and importance to them. An unexpected outcome has been educational benefit of much wider significance than the simple teaching of reasoning, as will become clear.

The major educational influence in the development of 'Philosophy for Children' is that of John Dewey (1900, 1902). To quote Lipman (1988):

> For surely it was Dewey who, in modern times, foresaw that education had to be redefined as the fostering of thinking rather than as transmission of knowledge; that there could be no difference in the method by which teachers were taught and the method by which they would be expected to teach; that the logic of a discipline must not be confused with the sequence of discoveries that would constitute its understanding; that student reflection is best stimulated by living experience, rather than by formally organised, dessicated text; that reasoning is sharpened and perfected by disciplined discussion as by nothing else and that reasoning skills are essential for successful reading and writing; and that the alternative to indoctrinating students with values is to help them to reflect effectively on the values that are constantly being urged on them.

Hence IAPC materials have been designed to further these ends, by promoting philosophical dialogue in the classroom. They provide stories rich in philosophical ideas, backed up by teaching manuals whose main purpose is to encourage speculation about these ideas. Whilst the freest possible approach is recommended in allowing children to choose topics and initiate discussion, it is the teacher's job to insist upon rigorous philosophical procedures in pursuing that discussion in order that it should not degenerate into mere idle conversation. Thus it should be expected that reasons will be offered for opinions, that assumptions will be examined, criteria suggested and clarified, and that a general aim is towards critical and self-critical awareness. The following discussion looks at some of the factors referred to in the above quotation regarding Dewey, and relates them to the use of the IAPC materials.

### Developing a 'community of inquiry'

That the dialogue takes place in a group setting is vital. Conceivably the group might be very small – half a dozen children or less – but in that case considerable advantages would be lost. A group of twelve to fifteen is considered ideal (though many teachers in the USA have been trained to work with their normal-sized classes of up to thirty). With a larger group there is a wider range of background experience and knowledge to feed the discussion. Also, there is likely to be a greater divergence of ways of approaching the discussion; some children tend to talk a great deal, others to remain silent, some to be disputatious, others seeking compromises between extreme positions, and so on. In order to carry on a discussion while these different influences are at work, children must inevitably learn something of the social skills necessary. It is the teacher's job to instil at the outset the importance of listening, in the active sense of paying close attention to what is said. It is not easy to get children to do this, given that traditionally the only person in the school they must listen to is the teacher. But to the extent that they become better at listening to each other they will not only get more out of the content of the discussion (and learn to reason better in the process), but become more aware of each other's differing attitudes and of what lies behind those differences. Lipman summarises this by describing the overall aim of 'Philosophy for Children' as the formation of 'communities of inquiry' in the classroom. The ultimate social importance of this idea could be immense. Its origin is attributed to the work of L.S. Vygotsky (1962), who compared children doing intellectual work co-operatively with those working in competition.

It will now be evident that the successful use of Lipman's materials to achieve these ends is far from easy. If there is any doubt about this, let us imagine a discussion in progress, and consider what different factors the teacher must be occupied with. While listening is important for the children, for the teacher it is fundamental to the success of achieving genuine discussion. It is only by the most careful listening that the teacher will become aware of the range of opinions on a given topic, and be able to devise questions to promote dialogue between the protagonists. Then there will be the need to consider which exercises from the manual would be useful for illuminating some idea that the children have raised; the need to remember fleeting contributions for future use, particularly if they raise further issues that need to be considered; noticing when the discussion has become side-tracked from the original question, deciding to what extent the side-track is worthwhile, and when the moment might be opportune for returning to the main topic. The prime motivation for these decisions is always what will maintain the children's interest and involvement. The teacher does not so much lead a discussion as facilitate its being led by the group. There is more. It is the teacher's job to notice mistakes in reasoning that are overlooked by the group, and devise ways of drawing attention to them; to insist that those doing the most talking are also prepared to listen, and to make sure that those who prefer to talk less have the opportunity to express themselves when they wish.

One measure of success will be the amount of talking the teacher has to do, which should be as little as possible. The more controversial and problematic the topic, the more it is likely to engage the children's interest, to the extent that they will often initiate dialogue between themselves; when this happens the teacher can and should revert purely to listening, coming in with a further question only when the children themselves seem to have reached an impasse.

This policy of non-intervention (as far as is possible) on the part of the teacher is fundamental to the educational approach advocated by the IAPC. Although lip-service is often paid to the notion of child-centred education, the practice of many teachers still owes much to the time-honoured model of instruction handed down from above. Perhaps this is not surprising when we consider that this is largely how they were themselves trained to be teachers. By contrast, the IAPC insists that learning is something actively undertaken by the learner, and that the only true teaching consists in initiating and aiding this activity. As a practical consequence, teachers undergoing training in IAPC materials are advised to restrict themselves to asking ques- tions, and never merely impart information. For example, suppose that during a dialogue some fallacy in reasoning occurs that nobody in the group notices. According to the usual model, the teacher should stop the proceedings, go to the board, and give a short lecture on the mistake that has occurred and how to avoid it. Quite possibly, by the time this has happened most of the children will have lost interest and be thinking of something else. Transmission of information is one thing; reception is quite another. But we can imagine an alternative way of proceeding: the teacher could refer back to the original remark where the mistake was made, and ask whether it really followed from what was said before. The group could argue a little about this, and as soon as somebody expresses doubt that it did follow, the teacher could ask, 'Well, why doesn't it follow?', and allow further discussion. In this way the children are discovering their own mistakes and attempting to correct each other. Genuine learning is taking place, and the point is much more likely to stick, because the learners have shaped it for themselves.

This non-instructional approach is by far the biggest stumbling block for teachers learning to use IAPC materials. To be successful at it they have to unlearn deeply ingrained habits. Restricting them- selves solely to questioning is itself difficult, but also they will have a tendency to ask the wrong kind of question – the sort that is directed to a specific answer the teacher already has in mind. The ability to ask open-ended questions comes with the ability to identify oneself as a co-inquirer with the children, to be genuinely puzzled by the sort of question that puzzles them. For, after all, philosophical questions *are* puzzling, which is precisely what makes them interesting.

Doing Philosophy with children is a practical skill, and can no more be learned from a book than riding a bicycle can. In recognition of this (and following Dewey), the IAPC insists that if teachers are to impart the skills of philosophical discussion to children, their training must itself consist in learning those skills by the identical method they will be expected to use. Teachers therefore attend seminars in which they are taken through the materials as a discussion group, the trainer modelling the role of teacher. Such seminars are not in themselves enough, but need to be backed up by work in the classroom with children. The trainer should visit schools to work with children for the teacher's benefit, and to observe the teacher for the purpose of giving individual advice.

*Critique and conclusions*

The original impetus for the development of 'Philosophy for Children' was the desire to improve reasoning ability. As we have seen, the full implications of promoting 'communities of inquiry' in the classroom go well beyond that somewhat limited aim, important though it is. Yet if we ask whether, over the years, 'Philosophy for Children' has proved to be successful, the concrete results we can point to concern only the reasoning element. The earliest attempt to test the effect of teaching *Harry* was carried out in New Jersey, not by testing the children's reasoning directly, but by comparing their school results in other subjects with those of the control group. The test results seemed to show a significant improvement, particularly in Mathematics and reading comprehension. Details of this and other tests can be found in the IAPC'S pamphlets, 'Philosophy for Children: Where We Are Now', *Thinking*, Supplements 1 and 2.

But as for the wider implications of introducing Philosophy into the school system in this way, we must rely upon evidence from interviews and questionnaires. These are also referred to in the above-mentioned pamphlets. In general, 'Philosophy for Children' has been well received in most parts of its country of origin, and in 1986 was granted 'national validation' by the US Department of Education. It has also attracted international attention, several countries having set up national centres for its dissemination, and where necessary translations have been made both of the reading material and of the teaching manuals.

Needless to say, an innovative educational venture of this kind has also been faced with various problems and criticisms. Not least of these is the cost of teacher training and of buying the necessary materials. In the USA this has usually been overcome by funding from grants from official educational bodies. Centres in other countries rely on similar kinds of funding. As yet, no means have been found in Britain of initiating any regular teacher-training in 'Philosophy for Children' of the kind outlined above.

If the experience in the USA is anything to go by, it seems that the success of training is very much dependent upon the teacher's understanding and acceptance of the IAPC'S aims, and enthusiasm for learning the kind of classroom methodology needed for their implementation. It would be ideal if training colleges were able to give instruction and practice in 'Philosophy for Children' to their students before the latter had developed habits in contrary teaching methods. This has not happened in the USA, arguably because colleges have, after all, a vested interest in traditional teaching methodology.

What of its acceptance by children? There is little doubt that on the whole they enjoy Philosophy sessions, given that the teacher knows how to have indicated that they appreciate the chance to say what they think about a wide range of issues. They enjoy the excitement of arguing their case against contrary views, and they appreciate the fact that in a community of inquiry they each have an equal right to be heard. For many children it is probably their first experience of being taken seriously as thinkers.

Interestingly, the few dissenting voices often come from those children who are clever in the traditional academic sense. They are puzzled and resentful when they realise that philosophical questions are not amenable to simple, straightforward answers – even from the teacher! Such children have unfortunately been trained to perceive educational value only in what can be examined and tested.

Regarding the materials themselves, children's reactions are varied. Part of the argument for using a story as a basis for discussion is the possibility of inventing characters with whom children can to some extent identify. But this demands considerable literary skill, which is hard to combine with the need for introducing logical and philosophical ideas. The problem is particularly evident in *Harry*, the first story Lipman wrote. Hence in some cases children have found the story itself tedious, though they have usually been willing to endure it for the sake of the discussion it gives rise to. Since such discussion is the ultimate aim, it may well be argued that the story is doing its job, and should be looked upon as a new kind of textbook rather than as a good read. It should also be noted that in later books Lipman has progressed a long way beyond *Harry* in overcoming stylistic problems, *Suki* and *Kio and Gus* being especially successful. But whatever problems there might be with designing the right kind of story, it seems to be an essential ingredient. Teachers have, on occasion, attempted to get discussion going by omitting the reading and using only manual exercises, but without success. Children seem to prefer a fictional setting to spark off their own thinking.

Another problem that has been raised is that of using American materials in other English-speaking countries. In Britain it might be thought that children are so familiar with American idioms from television, that this is hardly a problem in practice. But what is more important than purely linguistic differences is the cultural setting of the stories. In the long-run, it is probably necessary for non-American children to have a version more in keeping with their own background.

Further questions have been raised about the philosophical content. The IAPC recognises at least one major gap in the materials provided: there is no Philosophy of Science component for the middle and secondary school level. Specialists in other areas of philosophy will no doubt point to further omissions. But it should be noted that such omissions do not constitute a fundamental drawback. In principle, further components can be added indefinitely – the only requirement (admittedly no small one) being that other philosophers can match Lipman's skill in devising the necessary materials.

A more serious criticism, if it could be substantiated, would be that of philosophical bias. The possibility of such criticism has been mentioned by Reed (1987), who points out that notwithstanding Lipman's non-attachment to any particular school of philosophy, the whole curriculum is nevertheless by one author. It is true that any philosopher's work will exhibit special interests and influences. Can it be claimed therefore that 'Philosophy for Children' must inevitably encapsulate Lipman's philosophical viewpoint? No doubt, if another philosopher had produced the curriculum, we should find some different ideas appearing in the stories and in the teaching manuals; and ideas that Lipman has used might be approached in a different way. This is inevitable considering that a selection has to be made from the vast range of topics covered by Philosophy as a subject.

But given that the attempt is made to make the selection as representative as possible, the danger of any ill-effects occuring due to philosophical bias is minimised by the fact that the materials are not *taught* in any traditional sense. Their purpose is solely to elicit response from children, and it is that response which forms the basis for dialogue. Children are not encouraged to *accept* the philosophical ideas expressed in the materials; they are encouraged to *explore* them. (In any case the characters in the stories usually present opposing views.) Very likely the children's dialogue will throw up a range of alternative questions never even envisaged by the author of the materials. If the teacher correctly gives full attention to these ideas, allowing the group to discuss them critically, then even the most biased materials could be used with perfect safety.

To conclude this survey, I shall attempt to identify those aspects of 'Philosophy for Children' which make it significantly different from other approaches to the teaching of reasoning. The most obvious of these have already been discussed: the way in which Philosophy underpins the whole enterprise, both in regard to content and methodology; the use of fiction as a vehicle; and the development of 'communities of inquiry' through classroom dialogue. But what seems to me as important as any of these is the uncompromising insistence that children have a right to develop their own philosophical thinking. 'Philosophy for Children' will always be regarded with suspicion by those who would secretly prefer their children not to think, for fear that they might then have to do so for themselves. It will also disappoint those who hope for an educational tool for moulding children into some adult conception of what 'good thinkers' should be. Instead the boot is on the other foot, and we are urged above all to listen to children, tapping into the rich resources of their mental lives, and helping them to take control of their own thinking. In doing so, we may well make unexpected discoveries ourselves, not least about the nature of teaching.

*Bibliography*

Dewey, J. (1900, revised 1915), *The School And Society*, University of Chicago Press.

Dewey, J. (1902), *The Child And The Curriculum*, University of Chicago Press.

Institute for the Advancement of Philosophy for Children (1988), 'Philosophy for Children: Where We Are Now', *Thinking*, Supplements 1 and 2.

Lipman, M. (1988), *Philosophy Goes To School*, Temple University Press.

Lipman, M. and Sharp, A.M. (eds) (1978), *Growing Up With Philosophy*, Temple University Press.

Lipman, M., Sharp, A.M. and Oscanyan, F.S. (1980), *Philosophy in the Classroom*, Temple University Press.

Reed, R. (1987), 'Philosophy for Children: Some Problems', *Analytic Teaching*, Vol. 8 no. 1.

Vygotsky, L.S. (1962), *Thought and Language*, ed. and trans. E. Haufmann and F. Vakar, MIT Press.

Whalley, M.J. (1987), 'Unexamined Lives: the Case for Philosophy in Schools', *British Journal of Educational Studies* XXXV (3).

# 8: GETTING RESULTS AND SOLVING PROBLEMS

## K.F. Jackson.

*Introduction*

The ideas described in this essay follow a line of growth which draws from the work of J. Dewey, N.F. Maier, M. Wertheimer and many others. After working on problems in industry from 1953 the author developed a methodical approach to result-getting and problem-solving which he first taught to managers. In 1979 he set about introducing this subject into the curriculum of schools.

'Getting results and solving problems' is the name of a subject that one can study and put into practice. It is not one that can be said to be well known throughout the world of education, but there are many experienced practitioners of it today and there are substantial projects in progress to introduce it into the curriculum and into the management of the educational service.

The name 'Getting results and solving problems' was chosen so as to give as clear an indication of the nature of the subject as possible. Nevertheless, there is bound to be some possibility of misinterpretation and for making misleading assumptions on the basis of other uses of the same words, so it is necessary to examine its meaning with some care.

The results we are concerned with here are of any kind whatsoever. They may be results in school, such as learning how to calculate areas or achieving a performance of a piece of music. They may be results out of school, such as enjoying a walk or being helpful at home. They may be quantifiable, like test or football results, or unquantifiable, such as when one experiences personal satisfaction or when one's confidence grows.

The problems that the name of this subject refers to are the problems of life. They come into existence by occurring, and they occur to individuals and to organisations. They are situations in which progress towards an objective is thwarted by the presence of an obstacle. George Humphrey expressed the same idea in these words: 'A problem is a situation which for some reason appreciably holds up an organism in its efforts to reach a goal' (Humphrey 1951). For example, when pupils are trying to draw a plan of their school to scale they may find that they cannot make the distances add up properly. Or when they are trying to complete their coursework for GCSE they may find that having to do homework and revision for the examinations as well does not leave enough time. These problems are the ones that we all want to be able to solve, and they are the ones that we need to study and to learn from and to practise upon.

We need to appreciate that the word 'problem' is widely used in education and is often applied to things such as mathematical, scientific and constructional projects and exercises that do not have the same characteristics as the problems of life. These are not problems in the same sense, simply because in general they are free of thwarting obstacles. For many pupils or students they are tasks in which the level of difficulty is moderate and in which the way forward is reasonably clear.

The name 'Getting results and solving problems' reflects the need to get results in all circumstances, both when there is no obstacle to progress (no problem) and when there is one (a problem). It can be abbreviated to plain 'getting results', as it will be here and there in this essay, as long as it is understood that solving problems is a significant part of the subject.

The aim of education and training in any subject is to help the pupils or students to learn and thereby raise their accomplishments to the limit of their capabilities. In this subject the aim is to help all concerned to get the best results that they are capable of in any field. It is therefore a completely general subject, and in terms of school and college it is fully cross-curricular. It is normative. It does not attempt to be a descriptive subject or a branch of psychology. It is for learning what to think about and what to do in order to get better results, and not just for learning about how people usually behave when they want to get results.

*How can we get better results?*
In the longer term it may be possible to improve motivation, to increase knowledge, to increase self-confidence or single-mindedness, or to change any of the other factors that are capable of affecting results, but we cannot be sure either that these things will be accomplished or that they will have the desired effect. There is only one sure way to get better results, and that is to use better methods. It is nearly always possible to find a better method for accomplishing anything that we require to achieve, and once it has been found all that we have to do is to put the new method into practice.

All tasks that we need to accomplish, and all problems that we need to tackle, have much in common with each other in respect of the way we should think about them and set about dealing with them. Thus there are common methods that we can adopt for approaching tasks and problems. In the ordinary way we do not use these methods fully. We do not get the benefits that would come if we were to use them fully. So in order to get some of the better results that are available we do not need to go any further than to make sure that we use these common methods.

*Who knows about these common methods?*
The answer is that we all know about some of them, and that includes children as well as adults. Anyone who feels doubtful about this assertion can easily test it by asking people what we should think about when we want (a) to get a result or (b) to solve a problem.

*Where have the other methods come from, and what are they?*
In the course of history many thinking people have found better general ways of getting results and solving problems. In some cases their discoveries have come about when they have reflected upon successful work that they have done and then identified the method that it sprang from. In other cases a new way has been worked out in advance and then put to the test.

There is a large body of knowledge available to us in this field, from which we have to select. The scope of this essay is limited to the methods appropriate to an introductory course, and such a course can be adapted to the needs of anyone. Even the very youngest pupil at school can benefit from the simpler ideas, which in some cases are the most powerful.

The following list provides a syllabus suitable for an introductory course. It has been used for that purpose throughout the 1980s. It will remind readers of some of the methodical ideas that are already familiar to them, and may draw attention to some other items that hitherto they may not have thought about in this light.

*The essentials of 'Getting results and solving problems'*
To get better results:
1. Get your aims and objectives clear. Make sure that you know what results you want to get.
2. Work out how to get the results. Make plans and preparations. Develop a system for getting results you want, and gather and organise the resources that you need.
3. Take action and keep control. Monitor the quantity and quality of the results and the behaviour of the system. Compare with what

ought to be happening, and take corrective action.

4. As you get towards the finish, make sure that you complete the task properly and on time. Afterwards, review action, objectives, plans and preparations.

To solve a problem:

5. In every problem there is an objective and an obstacle. To solve it we must both achieve the objective(s) and overcome the obstacle(s). The way to do it methodically is to go stage by stage.

6. Five essential stages of problem-solving are:
a) Formulation.
b) Interpretation.
c) Constructing courses of action.
d) Decision-making.
e) Implementation.

7. Formulation contains:
a) Detection: we detect problems often through our feelings and emotions, or other people set problems for us. Detection means noticing that the problem is there.
b) Identification: classifying the problem or describing it.
c) Definition: only methodical problem-solvers take the trouble to define problems in terms of objective and obstacle.

8. Interpretation of problems is necessary in order to produce understanding or comprehension. We enquire or investigate in order to interpret. If the material that we do not comprehend is complex, analysis will help.

9. Analysis can be done in four steps:
a) List the elements.
b) Consider them.
c) Consider the relations between them.
d) Consider and evaluate the whole.

10. We need to record and show our comprehension by means of a description or model.

11. Constructing courses of action:
a) Set some general guiding principles, derived from objectives and results wanted, to which the solution should conform.
b) Plan strategically – broad principles first, details later.
c) Attend both to overcoming the obstacle and reaching the objective.

12. Creative work.
a) We need the right working conditions for us – such as some stimulation from others, and time-pressure.
b) We are all capable of creative work.

c) We need to think with:

i) Vision, which is seeing states of affairs in the imagination which do not yet exist in reality.

ii) Resourcefulness, which is seeing the value in that which we already possess.

iii) Ingenuity, which is needed for finding courses of action or ways and means of getting from where we are now to where we want to go.

13. Decision-making is for choosing what to do and for committing ourselves to action.

a) We ought to devise a system for making the decision if it is difficult or very important.

b) We need to identify some qualities which are relevant. These can be derived from our objectives and our system of values.

c) The qualities need to be assembled into a criterion for judging which course of action we prefer. If we want to select a definite number of courses of action, the criterion will involve putting the available alternatives in rank order. If an indefinite number, a standard to pass or fail will have to be set.

d) We need to measure or assess the qualities of the courses of action in terms which correspond to the nature of the qualities.

e) We need to apply the criterion and agree to carry out the preferred course of action which is identified by the criterion.

f) Decision-making sets a new objective which we will now pursue as a means to an end.

14. Implementation is the same as getting results.

*Rules and principles*

Most of the items in the above list are expressed in the form of rules or principles. Do we usually follow them or not? It is easy to find out. We can look back on the last time when there was an occasion to use any one of them and recall what actually happened. Or we can take any one of them, create a situation that calls for it, and see what we actually do about it. Or we can observe what happens when people are trying to get results, such as when they hold a meeting. More often than not we fail to follow what we well know is the right way to get better results.

To recapitulate, the first thing is to have a list of rules and principles that will lead to better results, and the next thing is to make sure that we follow them. The above list exists and is ready for use. It is an inclusive system. Any ideas that work can be combined with it at any time.

Following the rules and principles depends on understanding

them, on knowing when to apply them and when not, on knowing how to apply them, and on having sufficient self-discipline to see it through. Experience shows that pupils do not learn the majority of these things, some of which are theoretical and others practical, by the normal processes of education. Even if they did learn them eventually by the end of their schooldays, that would not be ideal, because the earlier they become proficient at getting results the more they learn from the curriculum in each year of their education. Changes in the present curriculum will be needed if we are going to make it happen, and provision will have to be made for teachers who wish to undertake this work to learn about this subject themselves in the first place.

## How to teach getting results

There are many ways to teach this subject. A way to be recommended is to ask the pupils what we should think about when we want to get results, and to put the list of their suggestions on view. Then, on the next occasion when they have to do something they can be obliged to put their ideas into practice and to judge whether they followed their own rules or not, and whether their actions were effective or not. From this basis they can gradually be introduced to the whole syllabus of the subject, always in the practical and real context of their normal course of study.

Apart from introductory text books for teachers, no extra resources are required. The basic materials are needs to get results and problems, which we have already.

## How it relates to thinking

Both in content and process, this subject makes use of some of the established knowledge about thinking. For example, in the case of creative thinking, where we have some understanding of the stages that a person may normally pass through when making a creative discovery, we should explain and demonstrate them to pupils so that they will know what to expect when they or others are involved in the discovery process. However, the subject as a whole is not conceived as a way of training the mind. It does not purport to show us how to think or what to think, but what we ought to think about in various circumstances.

To an extent it is like having a kit of tools for handling and shaping ideas. There are basic mental skills without which we cannot use any of the tools effectively. An example is being able to understand a simple rule and to follow it. Then there are higher order skills, which develop when we practise using the tools and become adept with them. An example of these is analysis. By practice in using a structured method for analysing any material that is too complicated to be understood fully by commonsense, analytical thinking can be facilitated and effectively improved. It is not claimed that such an improvement is accompanied by, or stems from, an enhancement of the underlying basic cognitive skills.

*Evaluation*

The effects of applying these ideas in the classroom by teachers and pupils can be judged in several ways. Over fifty teachers' reports on their own work can be seen in the pages of *Problem-Solving News* (see references). Two educational authorities have decided to incorporate getting results and solving problems into the curriculum of their schools.

The Dudley 'GRASP' project has an external evaluator, who writes as follows in her annual report for 1988:

> Pupils are reported to be better motivated and staff to have higher morale. Both have more confidence. The use of the GRASP (the Dudley project's name for 'Getting results and solving problems') approach, whether or not it is fully shared with the pupils, has had undoubted benefits by providing a working structure and a clear idea of the teachers' intentions. All pupils have benefited from knowing more clearly what is expected of them and having a recognised framework to work to. The best proof of this is where unclear objectives are set. The contrast of the resulting confusion with the 'good' GRASP lesson is very revealing. There is no doubt that GRASP is helping staff and pupils of all abilities to be more methodical and that this is improving the quality of the learning. (Jones 1988)

*Bibliography*

Humphrey, G. (1951), *Thinking*, Methuen.

Jackson, K.F. (ed.), *Problem-Solving News*.

Jackson, K.F. (1989), *Getting Results and Solving Problems in Education*. (Both published by the author at 16 Campbell Drive, Beaconsfield, Bucks HP9 1TF, UK.)

Jones, J. (1988), *Evaluation of Dudley GRASP Project*, Janet Jones Associates.

# 9: INSTRUMENTAL ENRICHMENT

## Bob Burden and Anton Florek

Instrumental Enrichment is a programme, developed by the Israeli psychologist and educator Reuven Feuerstein and his colleagues over many years, to help retarded performers become fully effective learners. It is worth noting the terminology used in this statement because it reflects some important aspects of Feuerstein's work and ideas.

Firstly, the use of the term 'retarded performer' is a useful one as it focuses upon the 'performance', leaving the person potentially intact in the labelling process – a feature which is still often lacking in our teaching culture today. Secondly, Instrumental Enrichment (commonly referred to as IE or FIE) is not primarily concerned with teaching 'thinking skills'. In fact, the term is something of an anathema to Feuerstein since he sees the purpose of his theory and methods as having a profound effect upon the underlying cognitive structures of all thinking and learning. In this sense, the teaching of skills can be seen as a peripheral activity which will only have a lasting and far-reaching effect if it is incorporated within a sound theoretical framework.

This point cannot be emphasised too strongly because it marks the essential difference between Feuerstein and most other producers of cognitive skills programmes. IE is merely the tip of an iceberg. It arises out of a belief system about human potential, a sophisticated theory of human learning, a revolutionary view of assessment and years of clinical and educational practice. In supporting such a position Feuerstein has argued that for him 'the chromosomes do not have the last word', alluding to the number of learners with Down's Syndrome in particular who have successfully participated in IE programmes.

The purpose of this chapter will be to elucidate some of the main aspects of Feuerstein's ideas so that IE can be understood within its proper context. A brief description of IE will then be given, relating it to these ideas and explaining Feuerstein's insistence upon proper training in what he terms 'the mediation process'. A résumé will be provided of some of the more important research studies into the effects of IE carried out across the world and some conclusions will be drawn about the importance of this work for teacher training and classroom practice.

## The roots of the theory

Reuven Feuerstein is a Rumanian Jew who was one of the founder members of the Zionist state of Israel after World War II. As one of the people responsible for the education of young people pouring into the new country from all corners of the world, he became aware not only of their culturally different backgrounds but also of the fact that many who were being categorised as mentally retarded because of what he terms 'cultural deprivation' or other reasons were potentially far more capable or 'dynamic' than was being revealed by conventional assessment techniques.

Out of this experience and his later work in Morocco, Feuerstein began to formulate a set of ideas which were quite revolutionary for their time. First, his definition of cultural deprivation is totally different from the once popular and now largely discredited notions of Bernstein and other sociologists of the 1960s. In Feuerstein's terms, culture should be seen as the active process by which knowledge, values and beliefs are transmitted from one generation to the next. Cultural deprivation is described as 'a state of reduced cognitive modifiability of the individual, in response to direct exposure to sources of stimulation' (1981, p. 15) which is the result of a failure on the part of a group to transmit or mediate its culture to the new generation. Further elaboration of Feuerstein's thoughts on culture can be found in one of his key early papers (1982).

The importance of this notion of cultural deprivation and its potential effects later on in life centres upon the fact that the most successful members of society and, for that matter, the most successful societies, are usually those who have access to their own cultures. Furthermore, knowing your own culture – having a sense of dignity and place within it – is surely the prerequisite to being able to adjust to or indeed assimilate another culture without losing your own identity. One of the primary tasks for parents and educators, therefore, must be to make that culture available to the child. Unless they do so, the children will fail educationally and cultures will ultimately die out.

Thus, a key issue for parents and teachers is how to teach children to learn how to learn and to understand themselves as learners in this process. For Feuerstein this became a burning question which subsequently led him to attack many strongly entrenched beliefs about human development; it also brought him into direct conflict with two of the most respected psychologists of their time, Jean Piaget and Arthur Jensen.

In his quest to gain a greater understanding of how children learn, Feuerstein moved to Geneva to study under Piaget; there he met and became impressed by the ideas of a less well-known psychologist Andre Rey, to whom he has always acknowledged his indebtedness. However, at a time when everything spoken and written by Piaget was being received unquestioningly by most child development scholars, Feuerstein came to believe that far too little emphasis was placed by the Genevan school on the social context of learning. In this he mirrored the, at the time largely unknown, idea of the great Russian psychologist Vygotsky and some of the later work of Jerome Bruner and others.

At the same time the fashionable views of Jensen and his British adherents, Burt and Eysenck, concerning the largely fixed and inherited nature of intelligence, ran counter to Feuerstein's developing views which focussed on the difference between intellectual potential and measured performance on IQ tests, and on the possibility of bringing about positive cognitive changes in even the most retarded individuals. On his return to Jerusalem and in his subsequent travels to North America and other parts of the world, Feuerstein began to build up a team of like-minded colleagues who set about funding practical ways of shattering some of these established myths. The most influential and enduring of those collaborators have been Jacov Rand and Mildred Hoffman and, later, Mogens Jensen. With initial funding from a group of Canadian Jewish women, the Hadassah-Wizo Research Institute was set up on the outskirts of Jerusalem: it became a centre for teaching, advice and support for teachers, parents and research workers from all over the world.

At a time when he was regularly dismissed as a 'crank' because his ideas were so out of keeping with current psychological dogma, Feuerstein began to travel the world speaking at international conferences about the remarkable changes that he claimed his team's ideas and methods were bringing about in the cognitive performance of individuals previously dismissed as 'unteachable'. To the world at large Feuerstein's growing reputation was only accessible by word of mouth or from brief conference proceedings, and it was not until the publication of two key texts – *The Dynamic Assessment of Retarded Performers* in 1979 and *Instrumental Enrichment* two years later – that his work and ideas became widely accessible. These texts are still essential reading for anyone seeking to understand the primary function of IE and its related assessment technique, the Learning Potential Assessment Device (LPAD).

*Important aspects of Feuerstein's thinking*

Feuerstein emphasises that ideas and theories do not grow out of nothing but are always based on values and belief systems. He sees such belief systems as fundamental to effective action and argues that without a belief in an almost limitless human potential, artificial barriers will always remain to prevent change. Thus he begins with the belief that all humans of any age, however severely disabled, from whatever cause, can become fully effective learners. He is not prepared to compromise on this. This view is clearly at odds with the still often held view that children with learning difficulties are coming to the classroom as static learners with fundamental disabilities which prevent any real access to change in their learning. Feuerstein views all humans as potentially dynamic; hence his belief in their potential for change. Given these arguments might it not be possible that we, in special education in particular and indeed in education generally, have severely under-taught generations of children by traditionally presuming that their ultimate ability to change is limited by their condition?

Once one is 'freed' by adopting such a belief system, a number of logical consequences automatically follow. Perhaps the key consequence for Feuerstein is his notion of 'structural cognitive modifiability' which is his way of saying that even the cognitive structure of the brain can be changed by enabling people to learn how to learn, in that learning becomes cumulative and in turn affects performance over one's lifespan. This, of course, runs counter to other traditional dogmas that we become less effective learners as we grow older. Feuerstein himself argues:

> The essential feature of this approach is that it is directed not merely at the remediation of specific behaviours and skills but at changes of a structural nature that alter the course and direction of cognitive development...'structural changes' refer...to the organism's manner of intereacting with, that is, acting on and responding to, sources of information. Thus a structural change, once set in motion, will determine the future course of an individual's development. (1981, p. 9)

The key to learning to learn lies in the notion of 'mediated learning experience' which is at the heart of Feuerstein's social interactionist theory of learning.

By mediated learning experience (MLE) Feuerstein refers:

> to the way in which stimuli emitted by the environment are transferred by a 'mediating' agent, usually a parent, sibling or other care giver. This mediating agent, guided by his intentions, culture, and emotional investment, selects and organises the

world of stimuli for the child...Through this process of mediation, the cognitive structure of the child is affected. (1981, pp. 15-16)

Much of the 'theory building' at the Jerusalem research institute has been directed towards explicating what is meant by mediation, and where and how it occurs. In some ways it the most fundamentally important aspect of Feuerstein's work but the least widely understood and acknowledged. Without mediation IE becomes just another thinking skills 'package' and the LPAD becomes an interesting set of diagnostic materials. Understanding these views is critical to using and evaluating Feuerstein's work in the classroom. Both of the present writers have been trained in using these materials, and it becomes increasingly clear with experience in using them that the concept and process of mediation in general and the teacher's role as mediator in particular are fundamental to producing a classroom culture of positive support to which all group members belong.

The three essential aspects of any proper mediation of a learning experience by a parent, teacher or care giver are that:

1. The mediator should be aware of, make known and ensure that the learner has understood what s/he is going to do (intentionality and reciprocity).

2. The mediator should explain why s/he is going to do it (investment of meaning).

3. The act should be conveyed as having value beyond the here and now (transcendence).

In describing the process of mediation Feuerstein suggests that:

An interaction that provides mediated learning must include an intention, on the part of the mediator, to transcend the immediate needs or concerns of the recipient of the mediation by venturing beyond the here and now in space and time. Indeed it is the intentional transcendent nature of the interaction that is the defining characteristic of a mediated interaction. (1980, p. 20)

A useful example of such intentional transcendence might be the scenario of two parties on the top level of a double decker bus, each party comprising one child and a parent. Looking out of the window child A says to parent A, 'Look, mummy/daddy, what's that?' Parent A looks up from reading a newspaper and says impatiently, 'It's a cow. Don't they teach you anything at that nursery school?' Further down the bus, however, child B asks the same question of parent B but gets the reply 'What does it look like? Tell me things about it. What colour is it? What is it doing?' Finally, after exhausting the immediate information about 'cow', the parent proceeds to elaborate and extend the child's knowledge beyond the immediate by discussing aspects of farming, milk and butter production, etc. The important differences are that child B has had a mediated learning experience within which she has been an active and dynamic participant. Child A on the other hand is little wiser to the concept of 'cow' than prior to the interaction.

The implications of intentional transcendence for children with special educational needs are clear if one accepts that all children bring a kaleidoscope of their own successful learning strategies with them to the classroom. All too often, however, the teacher fails to match what the child brings with what is required, thus preventing the child from sharing familiar aspects and concepts of her own culture within the learning situation of the classroom. It is this denial of cultural sharing which ultimately impedes the child in making sense of what is going on, thus causing difficulties in learning.

Other important aspects of mediation are as follows:

Mediation of feeling of competence.

Mediation, regulation and control of behaviour.

Mediated sharing behaviour.

Mediated individuation and psychological differentiation.

Mediation of goal seeking, goal setting and goal achieving planning behaviour.

Mediation of challenge: the search of novelty and complexity.

Mediation of an awareness of the human as a changing entity.

Only when all of these become an integral part of the teacher's repertoire, and are used constantly and appropriately, can true mediation be said to be occurring. A number of other aspects of mediation have also been described, and the interested reader is referred to the 1981 text for further details.

Bearing this in mind, it becomes clear that the effectiveness of any instigated IE programme will be largely dependent upon the quality of mediation – more even than the 'Instruments' themselves, although these are not unimportant. Any proper evaluation of IE should therefore concentrate as much upon the quality of the mediation process as upon pupil-centred outcomes. This also explains why Feuerstein is adamant that IE should not become a cheap and freely available 'package' but must be accompanied by intensive training and ongoing teacher support.

The final important foundation stone of both Instrumental Enrichment and the Learning Potential Assessment Device is Feuerstein's notion of the cognitive map. Basically, what this does is to identify the most important elements involved in the completion of any mental act. Seven key features are proposed:

1. The universe of content around which the act is centred.

2. The modality or language in which the act is expressed.

3. The phase of the cognitive functions required by the mental act.

4. The cognitive operations required by the mental act.

5. Level of complexity (including novelty and familiarity).

6. Level of abstraction.

7. The level of efficiency with which the mental act is performed.

The construction of both the LPAD and IE was directly related to each of these elements in a step-wise progression. Particular reference is made to the phase element within which the notion of deficient cognitive functions is introduced. It is argued here that in order to function effectively on any cognitive task information has to be gathered in an efficient manner (input), worked upon cognitively (elaboration), and any proposed solution must be expressed appropriately (output). A number of important ways have been identified in which these processes are disrupted or inefficiently performed. At the input level, for example, a person may act impulsively or in an unsystematic way or may lack the necessary verbal tools or spatial skills. At the elaboration level s/he may not see the need to pursue logical evidence, may lack strategies for hypothesis testing or may only have an episodic grasp of reality. At the output level s/he may only be able to communicate in an egocentric manner or again may not possess the necessary verbal tools to communicate adequately elaborated responses.

It follows that in identifying missing or inappropriate learning strategies in this way, we can also identify the kinds of behaviours that will foster learning. One of the most important functions of the LPAD is to identify a person's deficient cognitive strategies; one of the main purposes of IE, on the other hand, is to teach appropriate learning strategies and correct deficient cognitive functions. IE also aims to teach the concepts, operations and vocabulary necessary for successful problem solving, to develop motivation, to produce insight into reasons for success and failure, to foster successful work habits that will become both spontaneous and automatic, and to turn passive recipients into active generators of knowledge.

## The Instrumental Enrichment Programme

The term Instrumental Enrichment was deliberately chosen to represent the instrumental way in which the various activities are designed to enrich the cognitive abilities of retarded performers by means of appropriate mediation. The 'Instruments' can thus be seen as content-limited 'hooks' by which the teacher can introduce mediated learning experiences which can be generalised (or 'bridged') into academic or real-life problem situations. There are fourteen Instruments in all, which are usually incorporated into a lesson plan involving an introductory session setting out the aims of the lesson, a period of independent work on one Instrument, and a discussion period aimed at developing insight and principles for generalisation.

The Instruments are usually taught two or three times a week for 40-60 minutes per lesson over two years. It is common for two Instruments to be taught at any one time in consecutive lessons. The programme always begins with the Instrument known as Organisation of Dots which sets the scene for much of what is to follow. This Instrument is the most content-limited of all and often poses teachers a considerable challenge for this very reason. It is usually taught in conjunction with the first of the two Instruments devoted to spatial orientation. These are followed in the first year by Analytic Perception, Comparisons, Illustrations, Family Relations and Orientation in Space II. In the second year the Instruments become increasingly complex and abstract. Categorisation builds upon the work begun in the Comparison Instrument and is followed by Temporal Relations, Instructions, Numerical Progression, Syllogisms, Transitive Relations and Representational Stencil Designs. Examples of each of these Instruments are given in Howard Sharron's introductory text *Changing Children's Minds* and are described in full in Feuerstein's 1981 text.

### Does IE work?

There are now more than 100 reported studies into the effects of IE, carried out in several countries across the world and with a variety of different populations. The interested reader is referred to Burden (1987) for a review of this literature and discussion of some of the major difficulties faced by researchers in attemting to evaluate something as complex as IE with all its attendant aspects. A number of these studies show conclusively that performance on IQ tests is significantly affected by exposure to IE programmes. This has been found for educable mentally retarded, learning disabled, behaviourally disturbed, culturally deprived, deaf, brain-injured and disaffected students from the age of twelve upwards. Whereas most studies have tended to concentrate upon simple measures of student-centred learning outcomes such as IQ or attainment test scores, it should, however, be apparent to the reader that a far wider set of issues is involved. The quality of mediated learning experiences offered by the teacher, for example, will be absolutely crucial to any specific, or indeed general, learning outcome, yet this is rarely even mentioned. Significantly, both present authors have been involved in the organisation and delivery of a number of UK training courses in IE. What has consistently emerged from these courses is the qualitative change over time in teaching style produced in the IE trained teachers. As a result of these experiences IE awareness sessions are now incorporated on both initial and in-service courses presently directed by both writers.

Other important factors about which far too little is yet known are the culumative effect of IE over time, the minimum amount of input required to bring about change, the relative effect of various instruments and the most effective way of 'bridging' into mainstream curriculum areas. (An excellent 'Mediation Manual' devoted to the issue of bridging has been prepared by Ilg and Fisher at the Father Flanagan High School, Omaha, Nebraska.) Some studies have also shown positive effects on educational attainments, but it is clear that the quality of the bridging process plays a very important part here. Less striking are the measured improvements on self-concept tests, but interviews and observer ratings show clearly that students consider themselves to have benefited greatly from IE and that teachers who stick with it feel that their professional skills develop and that they enjoy teaching more.

*Classroom implications of IE*

In this chapter we have argued that Feuerstein's concept of mediation has a central role to play in promoting the active involvement of children in their own learning. The process of mediation promotes an acknowledgement of the fundamental dignity of the child within the learning situation. 'Bridging' enables the teacher to make sense of and extend what is happening in the classroom thus enabling the children to participate in the lesson on their own terms of understanding rather than the teacher's. Thus, the learners concerned become interactive participants in the lesson and in the process learn to reflect, hypothesise, seek information, listen to others, share in decisions and knowledge, and perhaps most importantly learn to acknowledge the individual differences which, far from dividing them, can be individually used to contribute to the collective wisdom of them all.

This process acknowledges a central role for the teacher as a dynamic filter for the new experiences that confront and confound children daily within the classroom environment. In this process the change in teaching style from transmission to mediation supports the development of a classroom culture based upon engagement and dignity within learning rather than disaffection and fear of failure – a feature of schools that has, for far too long, been part of the daily curriculum diet of children experiencing difficulties in learning.

*Bibliography*

Burden, R.L. (1987), 'Feuerstein's Instrumental Enrichment Programme: Important Issues in Research and Evaluation', *European Journal of Psychology of Education*, Vol. 2, No. 1, pp. 3-16.

Feuerstein, R., Rand, Y., and Hoffman, M.B. (1979), *The Dynamic Assessment of Retarded Performers*, Baltimore, University Park Press.

Feuerstein, R., Rand, Y., Hoffman, M.B., and Miller, R. (1980), *Instrumental Enrichment: an intervention programme for cognitive modifiability*, Baltimore, University Park Press.

Feuerstein, R. and Hoffman, M.B. (1982), 'Intergenerational Conflict of Rights: Cultural Imposition and Self Realization', *Journal of School Education*, Indiana University, Vol. 58, No. 1, pp. 44-63.

Ilg, J. and Fisher, M.B. (1987), *FIE Mediation Manual*, Father Flanagan High School, Omaha, Nebraska.

Sharron, H. (1987), *Changing Children's Minds*, London, Souvenir Press.

# 10: THE OXFORDSHIRE SKILLS PROGRAMME

## John Hanson

The Oxfordshire Skills Programme comprises a variety of initiatives designed to enhance children's thinking. Thinking in this context is defined as exercising the mind in order to make a decision. We need to think when we do not know, and thus have an opportunity to learn. Thinking may therefore be equated with problem-solving, and the Programme team readily accept the following diagram by Robert Ennis (presented informally at the Sixth International Conference at Sonoma State University, California, 1988) as a representation of the field:

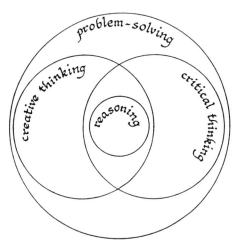

Each area of thinking is a concern of the Programme. Critical thinking is defined as disciplined thinking, in accordance with given or accepted principles, that is focused on deciding what reasonably to believe or do. Creative thinking is disciplined thinking that realises new problems, strategies and conclusions in focusing on what reasonably to believe or do. That which is reasonable exhibits conclusions drawn from and justified by evidence and sound judgement marked by moderation and a sense of fair play. Reasoning, at the centre of the field, represents deductive and inductive capability and the resolution of value judgements. Effective thinking exhibits all these qualities.

*History*

The roots of the Programme lie in the efforts in the 1960s and 1970s to develop skills of enquiry. In a number of subject development projects, locally and nationally, enquiry methods were associated with resource-based learning. In 1982 the LEA launched a Skills Project, using teacher secondments over two years to explore the feasibility of a more skill-based curriculum in secondary schools. There was in Oxfordshire an emphasis on classroom initiatives and local development groups rather than a total reliance on national projects. There was still, however, a failure to realise effective skills-learning or to introduce experiential in-service training.

*The Feuerstein experience*

In 1983 Oxfordshire successfully bid to take part in Sir Keith Joseph's Low Attaining Pupils Project (14-16), electing among other elements jointly with Somerset to pilot Reuven Feuerstein's Instrumental Enrichment. Six schools agreed to participate and to send two teachers on the first training course. The three-year pilot proved a valuable and formative experience in several ways: it illustrated clearly the value of underpinning classroom practice with psychological theory; it gave teachers insights into children's learning difficulties and an awareness of how children tackle problems. There were shortcomings: i.e. training lacked theoretical back-up and practice in mediation; the American material was not wholly satisfactory (being American in format and spelling, expensive and visually unattractive); the project evaluator's research findings were inconclusive. Certain objectives were not achieved: there was little evidence of skill transfer, and the teachers involved, like their skills work, tended to be isolated in the schools. Significant changes were noted in the social behaviour of many low-attaining students, including a rise in their self-confidence, which teachers valued highly. The experience was motivating to the great majority of teachers and students who participated, and this moved the Authority to extend development beyond the 14-16 age range and low-attaining population which LAPP prescribed. There was a consensus that the approach needed to be introduced at a lower age, and that it was relevant to the full range of ability. A whole-school and staff strategy was needed.

There were additional factors that gave momentum to developments in Oxfordshire. The Chief Education Officer was very supportive. The advisory service was involved in project leadership. The availability of a full-time designer facilitated the production of new materials. Teachers found support and partnership in local networks and in the classroom from project staff.

*A new programme emerged*

From these beginnings the Oxfordshire Skills Programme emerged as a separate project, to be adopted, wholly though modestly, by the Authority. It is concerned with developing children's effective thinking by a number of strategies, chief among which are an interactive methodology, a structured approach to skills-learning, and an emphasis on gaining insights into one's own ways of thinking.

Feuerstein's thinking remains central to the mediation of learning difficulties with low-attaining children: two Programme staff spent a week with Feuerstein in Jerusalem early in 1988. OSP is a significant influence in our Special Schools and this may be the first attraction to the many teachers from outside Oxfordshire who attend training workshops and use Programme materials.

In developing approaches for sixth form students in schools and colleges, mediation has a low profile and, particularly in relation to critical thinking, the project team have drawn on American experience, including the work of Richard Paul. This was faciliated by the participation of a Programme leader in the Sixth International Conference on Critical Thinking at Sonoma. A constructive dialogue has continued.

Exploring approaches at primary school level has led to interest in the work of Waldon, for example, and in the approach of Lipman's 'Philosophy for Children'. Primary development is a recent extension of the Programme, and the likely policy here is for the teacher to have command of a number of classroom strategies for effective thinking rather than one orthodoxy.

The programme has helped to inform the curriculum debate and the preparation of curriculum statements within the Authority. It aims to bring a coherent strategy on effective thinking across the 5-18 curriculum and in doing so to accommodate the sometimes contrary views of psychologists and philosophers. While academic debate continues, teachers need to assimilate and adapt ideas to the context of their classrooms and their students.

*A generic methodology*

The Oxfordshire Skills Programme represents above all a generic methodology for the enhancement of thinking in the classroom. It is this emphasis and experience which enables it to address the National Curriculum and to support teachers charged with its delivery.

Teachers who undertake the experiential training, and use that approach, tend to gain more insights into their own teaching and to act more effectively as problem-solvers. They are thus more aware of that sensitive balance between the means of learning, recognising when it is appropriate for children to rely on authority and when it is appropriate for them to make critical judgements, to think and work things through for themselves. The programme's methodology, being interactive, does not emphasise the teacher as authority in children's learning. It has the following attributes:

1. It values the mediating role of a teacher when a child is confused by a learning difficulty. It is subtle and sensitive intervention between the child's experience and the immediate task. Developmental, emotional, technical, environmental and social factors may inhibit the child's motivation and capability to think. Mediation should therefore be seen as a response to individual need.

2. It values the diagnostic role of the teacher which enables formative guidance. The emphasis in such assessment is not on finding what the child already knows, but why a problem has occurred and what are the next steps that may effectively be taken. (Vygotsky's zone of proximal potential is relevant here.)

3. It values discussion which encourages children to think, talk, listen and draw on their personal experience, modifying it in the light of new ideas.

4. It values problem-solving as the inherent curriculum discipline, in the sense that Popper suggested that human history is the story of man as problem-solver. It recognises the taxonomy of skill processes that begins with the finding and formulation of a problem, and leads through creative, critical and reasoned thinking to the justifying, testing and modification of a conclusion. It recognises the dynamic of the process. Overall, it seeks that organisation of experience for effective action which is the essence of skill.

5. It values knowledge as a vital prerequisite of enquiry and as experience which begs intelligent application.

6. Importantly, it values questioning as an invitation to thought and an implicit recognition of the child's right to respond to ideas, to express her own thoughts and formulate her own questions. Thus, in discussion the teacher constantly plays the ball back into the student's court. This is very different from conventional teaching, in which the great majority of questions asked concern recall or control. A friend last week told me of her daughter's complaint: 'I don't like it when our teacher asks questions because she always tells us the answer.'

7. It values language, both as a transparent medium for the communication of information and as a colourful medium for the evocation and expression of ideas, feelings and imagination. In this the teacher seeks to promote a common language for thinking across

the curriculum. Too often specialist terminology has inhibited the transfer of skill.

8. It values group activities which enable children to co-operate and learn from each other. Is there a better preparation for working life?

9. It values the child's response to classroom experiences, allowing him opportunities to express his feelings, to judge the purpose and effectiveness of his learning. This is helpful to the teacher's perception, and it leads also to children's personal statements which should be part of their records of achievement.

*The reflective teacher*
Do I :

give students a good range of opportunities to think and solve problems?

present work as problems to be formulated?

tell them what the problem is or ask them to decide?

encourage them to plan their work?

ask them to evaluate methods and evidence?

encourage them to look at sources critically?

help them to look for strengths and weaknesses in arguments?

ensure that they apply the skills and knowledge they have acquired elsewhere?

ask them to make judgements and reflect critically on what they have achieved?

give children the opportunity to communicate their ideas, experiences and feelings in a variety of ways?

encourage them to listen to each other?

encourage them to ask for clarification?

give ample time to group discussion?

call upon their imagination?

draw on their own experience?

encourage them to reflect on their classroom experiences?

give them opportunities to co-operate with each other and other people?

give them chances to develop social skills and attitudes?

allow individuals to support one another?

seek with colleagues a shared language of 'problem-solving'?

*A structure of skills*
Material and schemes of work recognise that familiar thinking processes comprise a number of cognitive functions or micro-skills. The most basic of these are perception, concept-formation, memory,

comparison and orientation, and they are constituents of compound functions such as classification and analysis. Enhanced performance at this functional level is likely to raise achievement at higher skill levels. Cognitive problems may often be tackled at the functional level. That is why much of the basic OSP material presents problem-solving in functional terms. Certainly when mediation of learning difficulty is at issue, subject content is a distraction.

A structured approach to learning can ensure a firmer mastery of thinking at a functional level which enables the child in due course confidently to meet higher demands for critical and creative thinking and the skills of 'the reasonable person'. How well can an A-level student tackle the task of comparing the foreign policy of two statesmen, for example, if she does not consider the parameters by which such a comparison makes relationships explicit? Too often in the past children have been confronted with problems and tasks without adequate guidance and preparation. It is now an issue with the introduction of National Curriculum programmes of study into primary schools. Much disaffection in the secondary school is arguably due originally to the introduction of work and textbooks which assume formal levels of thinking without the necessary support and guidance. The Programme aims to make this available. Materials are currently being designed to assist studies in GCSE, which has increased the external demand for skill-learning in the classroom.

*A political dimension*

There is a political dimension to any such programme. As John Newsom pointed out to parents forty years ago, 'until you have decided what the relationship between…man and other men should be, and what form of political and economic society you would like to see, you cannot tell what sort of education a child should have' (Newsom 1950, p. 12). Some right-wing groups now accuse schools of bringing up children to be sceptical; their opponents accuse such groups of requiring children to obey their masters without question and simply to place faith in their approved doctrines. But there is an intellectual integrity. Science, for example, should surely teach you to value doubt when evidence is unclear. And History?

A programme aiming to enhance children's creative, critical and reasoned thinking implicitly values a democratic society, and, since that term means many different things, let us say one in which the individual will be expected to act capably, freely, critically and reasonably. Those terms themselves need to be examined critically.

*The effective thinker*

A programme aiming to make children more effective thinkers must indicate what is intended, even if the result appears as a paragon of virtue.

The person who is an effective thinker will be:
1. Reasonable and fair-minded in judgement.
2. Considerate of other's views.
3. Efficient in problem-solving.
4. Enthusiastic in the pursuit of knowledge and understanding.
5. Independent of mind.
6. Self-aware.
7. Clear in communicating ideas and feelings.
8. Effective as a team member.
9. Critical in the evaluation of evidence and argument.
10. Creative.

*Research*

Research in this field is notoriously difficult. Commentators nevertheless tend to demand more evidence of achievement than they do of conventional subject teaching, particularly where the skills of effective teaching are taught in apparent isolation. Separate courses highlight the need for skill transfer, making explicit what is implicit and often overlooked in a subject curriculum. The Programme's stance here is that all the skills of effective thinking are inherent in the true discipline(s) of curriculum subjects, characterised by purpose (scientific, technological, humanistic or expressive) and the nature of the material/evidence. However, until all curriculum subjects exhibit a firm grasp of all that is thus involved, curriculum space should be found, preferably in tutorial time, when thinking itself is the focus of activity.

It is difficult to attribute gains in subject areas to activities conducted outside them. Who claims credit for a measured 10 per cent improvement in Maths performance over a short period? The telling evidence is likely to come from the perceptions of teachers and the students themselves rather than statistics. It is always an open problem. Closed, clinical research must always be qualified by its distance from the classroom.

While, therefore, limited teacher secondments have been used this year [1989] to investigate more closely the processes of mediation and the assessment of potential, Programme evaluation has been conducted generally through the recording of 'critical incidents', occasions when the teacher or a child was aware of a significant achievement or event attributable directly to 'thinking' lessons. It is a form of evidence that inhibits statistical analysis but it is valued by teachers and by parents when they are party to it. When a boy attibuted his exemplary conduct at the scene of a road accident to the discipline he acquired in OSP lessons, this was significant. When another student thought that the work had improved his golf handicap, I was more cautious.

There is another difficulty. The mental assimilation of new ways of thinking appears to take longer than normal periods over which testing is conducted. Feuerstein, for example, found the greatest relative advances were made after several years.

Experience has so far led us to believe that more is to be learned from classroom observation and dialogue with children than from standardised cognitive tests.

*What have we learned?*

A majority of teachers and students involved have been strongly motivated by OSP. Students report a greater ability to cope with problems and this has been exhibited most obviously in an increased self-confidence. Though this applies to the full ability range, it has been most evident among 'difficult' students, and perhaps least evident among those with marked linguistic ability.

Teachers report greater student achievement when they apply the Programme's approach to their own subject teaching. As most subject teachers are also group tutors, the involvement of OSP in the tutorial curriculum may be seen as one effective strategy for the transfer of skill.

We have learned that transfer of skill depends on a common language being available for problem-solving across subjects, on the disposition of students to approach problems and tasks in a disciplined way, on the students' experience of formulating problems successfully, and on the ability of staff to recognise and give signals that are significant in the processes of thinking.

We have learned much about the nature of skills and their characteristics in particular domains of the curriculum. But we still have a lot to learn and much experience remains to be gained in relation to skill transfer, whole-staff strategies for involvement, the needs of Primary children and the assessment of potential. With so many demands for change now upon teachers and a Programme team next year [1990] of only two leaders, with adequate resourcing but limited secondment facility, progress will not be rapid. The future of many such projects may be determined by their relevance to the National Curriculum and its delivery. I see the greatest relevance. I have been involved in curriculum development too long to claim that here is the panacea for all teachers' problems. On the other hand, too many teachers have volunteered that this experience has been the most significant influence on their teaching and thinking for me to deny that the Programme lies at the very heart of our professional role.

Why haven't we a national programme?

*Bibliography*

Newsom, J. (1950), *The Child at School*, Pelican.

Instrumental Enrichment:
    Craft, A. and Weller, K. (1983), *Making Up Our Minds*, Schools Council.
    Feuerstein, R. (1979), *The Dynamic Assessment of Retarded Performers*, Baltimore University Press.
    Feuerstein, R. (1980), *Instrumental Enrichment*, Baltimore University Press.

Oxfordshire Skills Programme:
    1987: *Teaching Cognitive Skills*, research paper, Oxon.
    1988: *Oxfordshire Skills Programme*, broadsheet, Oxon.
    1988: *Problem-solving Across the Curriculum*, Oxon.
    1988: *Asking Questions*, Oxon.
    These publications and further details are available from the Education Unit, Wheatley Centre, Littleworth Road, Wheatley, Oxford OX9 1PH (tel. Wheatley 2693).

# 11: THE SOMERSET THINKING SKILLS COURSE

## Nigel Blagg and Marj Ballinger

*Historical Context*

The Somerset Thinking Skills Course (Blagg, Ballinger, Gardner, Petty and Williams 1988a and b; Blagg, Ballinger, Gardner and Petty 1988a and b; Blagg, Ballinger and Gardner 1989a and b; Blagg, Ballinger and Gardner 1990a and b) is the result of a five-year curriculum development project, sponsored initially by the DES as part of the Low Attaining Pupil Programme. The project began in 1983 with the evaluation of Feuerstein's Instrumental Enrichment programme (Feuerstein 1980) which was systematically applied to over a thousand 14 -16 year olds in four Bridgwater secondary schools. 250 of these pupils alongside control pupils and 30 IE teachers together with 16 control teachers were carefully monitored over two years. A wide range of formative and summative assessment procedures were used involving many behavioural, attainment and cognitive indices. The detailed pupil and teacher findings are reported in Blagg (1991) and Blagg, Ballinger and Gardner (1990). A few of the salient features were:

There were significant changes in IE teacher attitudes, personality and classroom behaviour. IE teachers became more committed to teaching, more optimistic about the potential of 'low achievers' and more aware of their responsibilities in bringing about pupil change.

There were some welcome, positive shifts in pupils' attitudes and behaviour in IE classes.

There was very little evidence of any generalisable behavioural changes in the pupils and no evidence of ability or attainment changes.

Most teachers and pupils experienced extreme difficulty in relating the skills and strategies practised in the IE exercises to other curriculum areas and everyday life.

Nevertheless, the kinds of essential skills and strategies that IE began to highlight seemed fundamental to the cognitive demands of the changing secondary school curriculum. For instance, GCSE courses require pupils to study a wide variety of evidence, comprehend and extract information from it, notice gaps and inconsistencies, and detect bias. However, many pupils have been found to be lacking in the basic concepts, conventions, procedures and vocabulary necessary to cope with this kind of work. Teachers from many subject disciplines comment on pupil difficulty in using past experience to help them with a fresh problem. It is as though some pupils seem unable to recall and analyse previous tasks and compare them with a fresh problem to look for clues to help them. Teachers observe that some pupils do not know what it means to analyse or synthesise, or describe and compare; so how can they possibly make effective use of past experiences?

In view of these considerations, in 1985 Somerset set up a curriculum development group, led by Blagg, to produce a more contextually appropriate cognitive skills programme that would provide teachers with a carefully sequenced range of activities designed to help children to become better learners. The curriculum group brought together psychological expertise, experience of teaching cognitive skills and design proficiency. The outcome is the Somerset Thinking Skills Course.

*Aims and objectives*
The overriding aim of the Somerset Thinking Skills Course was to produce a set of activities, which if used according to the teacher guidelines and teacher training courses would enhance pupil learning ability. This was to be achieved by tackling a number of specific aims:

1. To enhance self-esteem.

2. To promote positive attitudes and beliefs about being able to learn to learn.

3. To heighten awareness of learning styles and the need to adjust them according to differing demands.

4. To enhance ability to communicate ideas accurately and clearly.

5. To teach basic cognitive resources underpinning problem-solving processes.

6. To develop awareness and control over the use of problem-solving processes.

7. To transform passive recipients of information into active searchers and generators of ideas.

8. To facilitate the ability to transfer and generalise ideas across many different contexts.

*Theoretical model*
There is overwhelming evidence to suggest that the extent to which children are active, optimistic and purposeful in their approach to learning and problem-solving will depend upon their previous learning experiences. Pupils who have experienced repeated failure in school

work, and have been constantly criticised even for their best efforts, are likely to have developed poor self-esteem. Many of these children will see little point in putting forward their ideas or making any effort in school tasks. Some will be only too willing to adopt the role of a less able pupil in preference to risking failure. STSC attempts to promote children's confidence and self-esteem in a number of ways:

1. The emphasis on establishing a safe, democratic environment in which pupils' ideas are carefully considered and valued, and where misunderstandings are handled sensitively and constructively.

2. The use of a wide range of novel discussion/problem-solving tasks that are relatively free from previous failure experience.

3. The inclusion of open-ended tasks where there are many alternative, justifiable interpretations communicating to the pupils that the teacher is not necessarily looking for correct or incorrect answers.

4. The provision of interesting visuals (pictures, cartoons, charts etc.) to stimulate and extend pupil ideas.

5. The careful sequencing of the pupil activities to allow for reinforcement and over-learning of basic skills, resources and strategies.

6. The emphasis on small group work and the development of oracy skills.

In relation to developing appropriate attitudes, beliefs and self-esteem there is also the need to consider pupils' learning style. Children often use particular learning styles irrespective of the problem or context. Many children with learning problems are impulsive (Kagan, Rosman, Day, Albert and Philips 1964), tending to rush into tasks before gathering appropriate information, often working in a trial and error manner and frequently recording ideas without sufficient attention to planning, accuracy or detail. At the other end of the spectrum, there are pupils who are over-reflective, constantly checking and re-checking information and plans so that they take an inordinate amount of time over tasks and often fail to finish. We provide materials within STSC to enable teachers to wean children off overdependency on inappropriate learning styles. Some STSC tasks demand very systematic, accurate and carefully planned responses, whereas others are more about brainstorming, risk-taking and the generation of many different possibilities.

Throughout the course there is a marked emphasis on encouraging pupils to verbalise their feelings, styles of working and particular problem-solving approaches. We promote the use of conscious questioning techniques related to two broad groups of teachable, cognitive skills:

1. Cognitive resources – specific skills and techniques.
2. Cognitive strategies – higher level control strategies concerned with the selection and coordination of resource skills for a particular purpose.

Nisbet and Shucksmith (1986) clarify the distinction between cognitive resources and strategies by using an analogy with a football team and its trainer. Individual players need to practise many skills, including heading, dribbling, ball control and so on. Prior to a particular match or at half time groups of players may plan certain tactics or strategies which involve a careful selection, sequencing and coordination of skills for a particular purpose. Nisbet and Shucksmith take the analogy further by querying what happens when the strategy does not work. A poor team might continue with the same tactics, irrespective of the outcome. A good team would be able to monitor and assess the situation, and flexibly adapt the strategy, to achieve the desired goals. It does not matter how proficient the individual players are at particular skills like tackling and sprinting if they cannot coordinate them into useful strategies. Furthermore, the analogy demonstrates that there are different levels of strategic thinking, with monitoring, checking and revising procedures requiring higher-level processes than generating and planning tactics. The problem for the trainer, like the teacher, is that of developing flexible strategic thinkers. While acquiring particular skills and techniques is an important part of educational experience, far more important is the business of developing pupil ability to select and flexibly *use* these techniques.

The cognitive strategies in the Somerset working model (see figure, p. 115) represent the higher-level general control processes concerned with selecting and coordinating specific cognitive resources for a particular goal. Although there is no commonly agreed taxonomy of cognitive strategies, there is general consensus about the important domains:

1. Gathering and organising relevant information.
2. Recognising and defining the problem.
3. Generating alternative solutions.
4. Planning tactics.
5. Monitoring performance.
6. Checking performance against original goals.
7. Revising plans and strategies to meet original goals.
8. Evaluating performance and strategies.

These areas commonly feature in problem-solving loops in a variety of curriculum areas. However, STSC has also included as separate domains:

9. Communication.

10. Transfer and generalisation.

Communication is highlighted because of the need to recognise the importance of having the kinds of language skills effectively to manage all of the other problem-solving domains. For instance, there is the need for particular kinds of language skills to describe, compare, hypothesise, explain, evaluate, justify and so on. Transfer and generalisation is perhaps the most fundamental issue facing teachers. It is not enough to teach children particular techniques or procedures. What is far more important is to teach them how to select and apply techniques and procedures to suit fresh problems. This issue will be returned to towards the end of the chapter.

Each of the strategy domains in the working model can be unpacked into 'sub-strategies' so that we can more clearly appreciate what is involved in applying cognitive strategies. For instance, recognising and defining problems might involve the following kinds of strategies:

| *Domain* | *Examples* |
|---|---|
| Recognising and Defining | Asking questions to clarify the problem |
| | Exploring implicit and explicit instructions |
| | Using previous knowledge/experience |
| | Analysing the problem into its constituent parts |
| | Systematically searching and checking the data |
| | Translating the problem into a task with clear goals |
| | Selecting and organising relevant information |

Strategies can be ordered into a hierarchy so that those within the domain of recognising and defining problems, or planning, form a continuum with higher-level strategies in the domains of monitoring, self-testing and evaluating. Strategies in these latter areas required more conscious awareness of cognitive processes – an area of self-knowledge referred to in the psychological literature as 'meta-cognition'. Metacognitivists like Flavell (1976) and Campione, Brown and Ferrara (1982) argue that if pupils can become more consciously aware of their thought processes when solving problems, this may in turn lead to better control over these same processes. They note that young children and low achievers are less able than adults or high achievers to talk about techniques and methods of problem-solving and learning employed in specific tasks.

Unfortunately, many children operate on a limited repertoire of strategies because they do not possess the prerequisites necessary to think strategically.

For instance, solving a problem by analogy with a related previous experience involves many cognitive elements, including the ability to analyse, synthesise, describe and compare. Issues like these we have subsumed under the heading of cognitive resources which are shown at the 'hub' of the STSC model (see figure, p. 115). Once again, there is no universal agreement on which resources are the most important, and the list of competing items is extensive. We have tended to include many areas highlighted by Feuerstein in his 'deficient cognitive functions list', but in addition we have included other items that have an obvious face validity in relation to many secondary school curriculum areas. STSC cognitive resources can be divided into four main domains as listed below:

| Domains | Examples | Purpose |
|---------|----------|---------|
| 1. Conceptual Understanding | Of number, space, time etc. | To build a coherent, stable model of the world |
| 2. Skills and Procedures | Scanning and focusing analysis and synthesis | To process, organise, memorise and retrieve information |
| 3. Knowledge and Experience | Of codes and symbols, conventions and rules etc. | To interpret and represent information in many different modes |
| 4. Linguistic Tools | Vocabulary and terminology, language registers etc. | To understand and apply language in its many different forms, functions and varieties |

*Structure and organisation of the course*
STSC involves a series of visually based discussion tasks around modular themes organised to suit a spiralling linear model graded in difficulty. Each module revisits and builds on ideas, principles and strategies established earlier, and continually checks for pupil knowledge and use of important cognitive resources. The complete course includes a handbook and eight modules:

1. **Foundations for Problem-Solving** – sets the scene for all

subsequent modules. It establishes the aims, format and conventions of the course. It concentrates on a range of procedures and skills essential to gathering and organising relevant information and recognising and defining problems. For instance, pupils are taught to scan and focus; distinguish between explicit and implicit information; use systematic search strategies; describe and label essential features.

2. **Analysing and Synthesising** – develops important vocabulary, concepts, skills and strategies introduced in the Foundations module, but focuses more specifically on the nature of analysis and synthesis in everyday life. Pupil activities consider part-whole relationships in both structures and operations and link understanding in this area to different forms of instructions, error analysis and design issues. The final stages of the module lead on to an appreciation of the interrelationships between structure, function and aesthetic considerations.

3. **Positions in Time and Space** – heightens pupil awareness of the way in which temporal and spatial considerations lie at the heart of planning and anticipating. The module exposes and integrates key concepts and vocabulary relating to reference points in time and space. Analytic behaviour is now enhanced with specific spatial labelling systems and is given a past-present-future dimension.

4. **Comparative Thinking** – focuses on the distinction between describing and comparing before developing the nature, meaning and purpose of comparison, utilising a wide variety of contexts and problem-solving situations. It explores the contribution spontaneous comparative behaviour makes to all kinds of decision making. The later stages of the module demonstrate how comparison forms the basis of classification. The nature and purpose of classification is explored and related in a variety of ways to both subject matter and social organisations.

5. **Understanding Analogies** – explores the nature of symbolism and analogy in everyday life. The module considers comparative principles involved in understanding a wide range of transformations and relationships (pictorial, figural and cartoon). It goes on to show how transformations form the basis of understanding different kinds of analogies and how analogy, metaphor and simile are related.

6. **Patterns in Time and Space** – explores the kinds of predictions one can make from understanding patterns and relationships in time and space, like cyclical rhythms, speed and momentum. The later stages of the module broaden the activities beyond physical issues into 'mental' issues. In particular, the module considers how different people come to adopt very different 'mental positions' or viewpoints. This involves exploring the nature of empathy and prejudice.

7. **Organising and memorising** – revisits many of the ideas and

resources emphasised in previous modules, with an explicit focus on techniques and strategies to facilitate recalling, organising and memorising different types of information. The module emphasises flexible strategic thinking through tasks which prompt pupils to consider which types of organising and memorising techniques and resources should be used for different purposes.

8. **Predicting and Deciding** – integrates and summarises aspects from previous modules in the context of a wide range of social, domestic and academic decision-making activities. It highlights the fact that most decision making is based on probabilities rather than certainties. It encourages pupils to consider how different kinds of evidence and information contribute to probabilistic thinking.

Within each module there are open-ended and closed tasks varying in complexity and presentation modes. These tasks can be separated into three types:

a) **Stimulus Activities** – are small group discussion tasks which establish a meaningful context and theme as a backcloth to the rest of the activities in each module. They broaden pupil learning by offering numerous opportunities to explore connections and associations between different areas of experience. These tasks are quite complex and involve open-ended activities that foster and encourage imaginative and divergent interpretations which need to be justified by reference to the information provided.

b) **Artificial Tasks** – are contextually bare activities that expose, teach and practise particular cognitive resources. Some of the tasks are 'closed' and require a very focused serialistic approach to find one particular solution, whereas other tasks are more 'open-ended' and ambiguous with many alternative interpretations and solutions.

c) **Naturalistic Tasks** – involve problem-solving tasks that relate to everyday life, enabling teachers to check for literal and figural transfer of resources exposed and practised on the artificial tasks. These tasks offer the teacher the chance to mediate at a macro- and a micro- level by identifying: (i) pupils who can demonstrate knowledge of numerous cognitive resources but remain unable to select and deploy them in appropriate problem-solving contexts; (ii) pupils who experience strategic difficulties because they still have major gaps in their cognitive resources.

*Transfer and generalisation*

Transfer and generalisation issues are addressed from three perspectives: the structure and organisation of the programme; the behaviour of the teacher; and timetabling and cross-curricular issues. The programme has a strong metacognitive focus, with pupils being encouraged to think about their thinking and summarise the skills and strategies they have used in each activity. The course holds that developing self-knowledge of problem-solving heuristics is a necessary, although not sufficient, condition for coping with fresh problems. Beyond this, the pupils' activities and teacher guidelines provide a continuum of transfer possibilities:

1. Each STSC task is preceded by an introductory activity which should contextualise the task for the pupils. The STSC exercise then provides an immediate opportunity to check pupil ability to transfer ideas and processes (either literally or figurally), i.e. teachers can note whether pupils do see the link between the introduction and the STSC exercise.

2. The development phase of each lesson relates the skills and strategies involved to other contexts through inductive and deductive questioning, e.g. 'Where have you met this or a similar problem before?', 'Where else might you use these skills?'

3. Each lesson ends with a summative review in which the teachers provide examples of transfer (near and/or far, literal and/or figural, depending on pupil ability and the nature of the task). Naturally, pupils are given the opportunity to offer their own examples of transfer and, indeed, spontaneous transfer is expected as the course progresses. Wherever possible, examples of figural transfer are formalised into generalisations.

4. Within each module the use of different task types, in varying levels of complexity and across different modes, provides a rich range of contexts to look for, and, if necessary, to point out examples of literal and figural transfer. At strategic points, mastery activities are included that extend the range and level of transfer demands.

5. The increasing complexity and abstraction that builds throughout the course necessitates the transfer of ideas and principles from earlier to later modules.

The importance of teachers developing a Socratic dialogue in which pupils learn to question critically and reflect on their own ideas and those of others, has already been discussed. Naturally, the course recognises that some pupils may feel threatened by too many open-ended questions and demands, or they may simply not have the resources to cope with them. Accordingly, we advise – 'mediate as little as possible and as much as necessary', but with a constant emphasis on high expectations and sufficient time for children to think through and justify their own ideas. It is all too easy to simplify problem-solving tasks in school when realities of the real world, like selecting the best value-for-money shampoo from a supermarket, involve massive complexity.

Finally, transfer and generalisation is unlikely to occur if cognitive skills work is treated as a 'bolt on' activity. STSC needs to be constructively integrated with other curriculum areas so that pupils can be prompted and guided to use the skills and strategies developed in the course in a range of classroom environments and subject areas. In practice, this means flexible timetabling involving integrated studies, cross-curricular modules and extensive INSET for subject specialists so that they can appreciate the links between STSC and the cognitive demands of the National Curriculum core and foundation subjects.

## Applications

During the piloting phase the materials were applied to all ages and ability ranges within secondary education, and small scale investigations were conducted with top primary children and further education students. There has also been considerable interest from the industrial world. There is scope for the materials in many different contexts provided they are properly understood and appropriately used. The majority of the activities can be interpreted at varying levels of sophistication.

At the top primary level, for example, the work fits very well with other investigative and problem-solving type activities, in addition to linguistic work designed to develop pupils' oracy skills. At the secondary level, many teachers have identified the course as an essential prerequisite for the GCSE. The work has been highly successful with mixed ability first year pupils. One pilot school allocated three of its five 50-minute Humanities lessons to STSC on the basis that the issues addressed in STSC were fundamental to Humanities work. It was interesting that two groups of pupils who received STSC in this way performed much better in the remaining two periods of Humanities than a third group who received their full quota of Humanities lessons.

Other pilot schools have established cross-curricular links by timetabling STSC within English, Maths and Environmental Studies. A number of schools have demonstrated the usefulness of STSC as part of an integrated modular course for fourth and fifth year pupils. At a more intensive level, the work has been usefully applied to special needs pupils of all ages.

## Effectiveness

Lake (1989) studied the effects of STSC with mixed ability third and fourth year pupils over one term. There were two STSC groups. One was presented with Foundations for Problem-Solving activities with no emphasis on metacognition, discussion and mediation: the other group was presented with the same materials but in the more reflective, discussion-oriented style intended by the originators. Whereas the first group showed no significant transferred improvement other than a reduction in rating for impulsivity, the second group revealed significant improvements in learning attitudes and general adjustment that continued beyond the STSC classes and the life of the project.

A number of other major studies are underway, looking at teacher and pupil change across a range of parameters. However, substantial anecdotal, observational evidence has already been gathered, pointing to the efficacy of the programme. Typical teacher comments include:

'First year pupils took to the work very quickly and the quality of the discussion frankly took me by surprise. Pupils with quite severe deficits in basic skills revelled in the discussions. These children were also being taught in a mixed ability setting for some other subjects, and by Christmas some members of staff were noticing their unusual forwardness in discussion work, even by comparison with the brightest pupils.'

'The Course has helped to move staff away from their chalk and talk approach. The pupils like the materials and saw much that teachers missed. Questioning techniques show improvement. In the Thinking Keys activity (Foundations module), children nailed down the details very rapidly and showed a fantastic understanding for the cartoons. They now use the page spontaneously when discussing the skills they have been using.'

'There's a very positive response to the Course. STSC is for us primarily a diagnostic tool that has highlighted problems that we should have been aware of ten years ago!'

*Bibliography*

Blagg, N.R. (1991), *Can We Teach Intelligence? A Comprehensive Appraisal of Feuerstein's Instrumental Enrichment Programme*, New Jersey: Lawrence Erlbaum Associates.

Blagg, N.R., Ballinger, M.P., Gardner, R.J., *Teaching Thinking Skills*, Routledge, in preparation.

Blagg, N.R., Ballinger, M.P., Gardner, R.J., Petty, M. and Williams, G. (1988a), *The Somerset Thinking Skills Course – Foundations for Problem Solving*, Blackwell Education.

Blagg, N.R., Ballinger, M.P., Gardner, R.J., Petty, M. and Williams, G. (1988b), *The Somerset Thinking Skills Course – Analysing and Synthesising*, Blackwell Education.

Blagg, N.R., Ballinger, M.P., Gardner, R.J. and Petty, M. (1988a), *The Somerset Thinking Skills Course – Comparative Thinking*, Blackwell Education.

Blagg, N.R., Ballinger, M.P., Gardner, R.J. and Petty, M. (1988b), *The Somerset Thinking Skills Course – Positions in Time and Space*, Blackwell Education.

Blagg, N.R., Ballinger, M.P. and Gardner, R.J. (1989a), *The Somerset Thinking Skills Course – Understanding Analogies*, Blackwell Education.

Blagg, N.R., Ballinger, M.P. and Gardner, R.J. (1989b), *The Somerset Thinking Skills Course – Patterns in Time and Space*, Blackwell Education.

Blagg, N.R., Ballinger, M.P. and Gardner, R.J. (1990a, in preparation), *The Somerset Thinking Skills Course – Organising and Memorising*, Blackwell Education.

Blagg, N.R., Ballinger, M.P. and Gardner, R.J. (1990b, in preparation) *The Somerset Thinking Skills Course – Predicting and Deciding*, Blackwell Education.

Campione, J.C., Brown, A.L. and Ferrara, R.A. (1982), 'Mental Retardation and Intelligence', in Sternberg R.J. (ed.), *Handbook of Human Intelligence,* Cambridge University Press.

Feuerstein, R. (1980), *Instrumental Enrichment: An Intervention Programme for Cognitive Modifiability,* Baltimore: University Park Press.

Flavell, J.H. (1976), 'Metacognitive Aspects of Problem Solving', in Resnick, L.B. (ed.), *The Nature of Intelligence*, Hillsdale, New Jersey: Erlbaum.

Kagan, J., Rosman, B.L., Day, D., Albert, J. and Philips, W. (1964), *Information Processing in the Child: Significance of Analytic and Reflective Attitudes*, Psychological Monographs, 78. Whole No. 578, 1964).

Lake, M. (1989), 'Mind Games in Milton Keynes', *Special Children*, March, 1989.

Nisbet, J. and Shucksmith, J. (1986), *Learning Strategies*, Routledge and Kegan Paul.

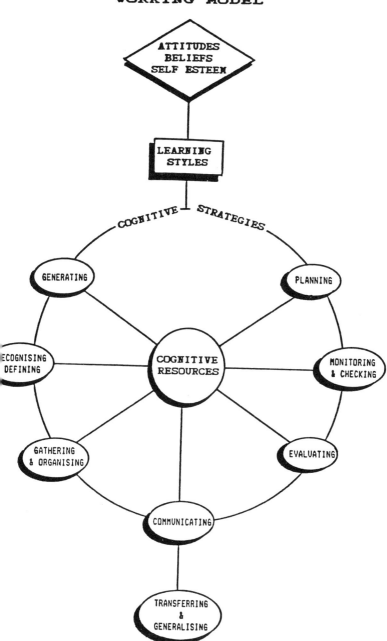

SOMERSET THINKING SKILLS
WORKING MODEL

# CONTRIBUTORS

**Marj Ballinger** is a History and English teacher who has taught throughout the secondary age and ability range. She has extensive experience of teaching English as a foreign language in many countries overseas and is currently seconded to the team developing the Somerset Thinking Skills Course.

**Nigel Blagg** is a senior educational psychologist currently seconded from his normal LEA duties to lead the development of the Somerset Thinking Skills Course. He graduated in Psychology at Nottingham University, where he took his Masters degree in child psychology before going on to do his doctorate in the treatment of school refusal at the Institute of Psychiatry, University of London. Dr Blagg has researched and published extensively on learning and emotional difficulties in childhood.

**Robert Burden** obtained his BA in Psychology at the University of Hull and his PhD – on the effects of early intervention with families of handicapped children – at Exeter University, where he has been Senior Lecturer in Educational Psychology since 1982. He has been an admirer of Reuven Feuerstein's work for many years and has received training in both the LPAD and IE in Jerusalem.

**Martin Coles** trained as a teacher and for a number of years taught in primary schools in Zambia and Oxfordshire, which time included a period as a headteacher. His interest in teaching thinking originated in studies he undertook at the London Institute of Education. He has been a lecturer in Education at Portsmouth Polytechnic, where he was involved in a project to introduce schools to Philosophy for Children and he now holds a similar post at the University of Nottingham.

**Alec Fisher** lectures on Philosophy and Logic at the University of East Anglia, Norwich. He organised the First British Conference on Informal Logic and Critical Thinking, and edited its *Proceedings* (UEA 1988). He recently published a book aimed at teaching university students to reason well (*The Logic of Real Arguments*, Cambridge University Press 1988). He has published several articles on critical thinking and has lectured on the subject in Britain, Holland, Canada and the United States. He is currently researching for the University of Cambridge Local Examinations Syndicate into tests of reasoning skills.

**Anton Florek** is currently Tutor-in-Charge of Special Educational Needs Courses at the North East Wales Institute of Higher Education, Wrexham. Prior to this he was Co-ordinator of Special Educational Needs at Connah's Quay High School, Clwyd. During the past few years he has become increasingly involved in school- based in-service work and has been responsible for organising many teacher /school/LEA-based courses in addition to co-directing DES regional courses and the annual Chester Summer and Easter Schools in Special Educational Needs. He is Visiting Lecturer in Special Educational Needs at University College, Bangor, where he directs a module on the part-time Masters degree course. He is also Visiting Lecturer at Liverpool Polytechnic and, in conjunction with Bob Spalding, is currently working in six LEAs on school-based in-service initiatives. He has published a number of articles and papers in the field of Special Education Needs and, with Mel Ainscow, is co-editing *Whole School Approaches to Meeting Special Educational Needs*, soon to be published by David Fulton, NCSE. At the present time he is co-ordinating two research projects for the University of Wales.

**John Hanson** had a variety of teaching experience both in England and overseas before taking up an advisory post in Oxfordshire some twenty years ago. This has involved a range of responsibilities, including the directing of the Low Attaining Pupils Project. After piloting the Instrumental Enrichment trials in the county, he led the team which developed the Oxfordshire Skills Programme. He has led a number of British Council Teacher Education visits to Africa, is the author of several educational books, best known of which are the *Enquiries* series published by Longmans, and has been a cartoonist for the journal *Education*.

**Greg Hunt** graduated in Mathematics and Physics, working briefly as an aeronautical engineer before his graduate degree in History and Philosophy of Science. He now lectures in the Department of Philosophy, University of Warwick, teaching Logic and the Philosophy of Science and of Psychology. His research work is in artificial intelligence and general Philosophy of Science. He is Editor of the *British Journal for the Philosophy of Science*.

**Keith Jackson** is an engineer and psychologist. After national service in the REME he worked on problems of many kinds in military and civil aviation for nineteen years. He was a research officer and member of the directing staff at Henley for seven years and then directed the Bulmershe-Comino Problem-Solving Project for nine years. He is now an independent consultant and his work is devoted to the promotion of the study of Getting Results and Solving Problems in schools. Author's address: 16 Campbell Drive, Beaconsfield, Bucks, HP9 1TF.

**John Nisbet** is a Senior Research Fellow in the Department of Education at the University of Aberdeen, having been Professor there from 1963 to 1988. He also held Visiting Professor appointments in Australia, New Zealand, California and Illinois. He was President of the British Educational Research Association (1975), Chairman of the Educational Research Board of the Social Science Research Council (1972-5), Chairman of the Scottish Council for Research in Education (1975-8), Editor of the *British Journal of Educational Psychology* (1968-74), Editor of *Studies in Higher Education* (1980-4) and Joint Editor of the 1985 *World Yearbook of Education*. In 1989-90, he was Consultant to OECD for the programme on 'Learning to Think – Thinking to Learn', and his publications include *Learning Strategies* and review articles on teaching thinking in scientific journals.

**Dermot O'Keeffe** was born in 1958 and studied Philosophy at University College London. He took his PGCE at Cambridge and taught at St George's College, Weybridge, then becoming Head of Philosophy and Senior Arts Tutor for the Sixth Form at Trinity School, Leamington Spa. He is a member of the Philosophy panel of the Associated Examining Board.

**Humphrey Palmer** grew up in Yorkshire and studied in Oxford. He has taught at two colleges in India and at University College in Cardiff, dealing mainly with the logical and metaphysical traditions of both countries. He worked with Dr D.M. Evans and others to launch the Cardiff 'Logic in Schools' project (as described in his chapter), for which they wrote the text *Understanding Arguments*, now also used in universities.

**Will Robinson** has been a senior lecturer in Philosophy of Religion both in West Africa and Britain. As Leverhulme Trust Research Fellow and Visiting Fellow, Department of Philosophy, Warwick University, he widened his interest to the teaching of effective thinking at all levels. He has been a presenter at a number of International Conferences on Critical Thinking in California and at the First British Conference on Critical Thinking in 1988. He is a recognised trainer in 'Philosophy for Children' and now concentrates full time on his business 'Developing Effective Thinking'.

**M.J.Whalley** is a British philosopher and an Associate of The Institute for the Advancement of Philosophy for Children in New Jersey, USA. For several years he worked as a teacher trainer for the IAPC. At present he is employed as a Philosophy teacher at an international school in Ecuador.